AL SIRAJIYYAH

AL SIRAJIYYAH

OR THE MOHAMMEDAN LAW OF INHERITANCE

ALMARIC RUMSEY

GYAN

Published by

GYAN

Gyan Publishing House
5, Ansari Road
Darryaganj, New Delhi-110002
Phone: 011-47034999, 9811692060
E-mail: books@gyanbooks.com

Distribution Network
gyanbooks.com
India, USA, Canada, UK, Australia

ISBN: 978-93-7414-210-3 (PB)

First Published, 1869

2nd Impression 2026

Printed at: Gyan Press, Delhi.

AL SIRAJIYYAH
Author: ALMARIC RUMSEY

AL SIRAJIYYAH:

OR THE

Mahommedan Law of Inheritance.

REPRINTED FROM

THE TRANSLATION OF SIR WILLIAM JONES,
PUBLISHED AT CALCUTTA IN 1792.

WITH NOTES AND APPENDIX

BY

ALMARIC RUMSEY,

BARRISTER-AT-LAW.

Member of the Royal Asiatic Society; Author of "A Chart of Family Inheritance, according to Orthodox Moohummudan Law, with an Explanatory Treatise;" "A Chart of Hindu Family Inheritance, with an Explanatory Treatise," &c.

LONDON:
WILLIAM AMER, LINCOLN'S INN GATE,
Law Bookseller and Publisher.

1869.

TO

ILTUDUS THOMAS PRICHARD, Esq.,

BARRISTER-AT-LAW,

THROUGH WHOM THE AUTHOR'S ATTENTION WAS FIRST DIRECTED TO THE STUDY OF INDIAN LAW,

This Work

IS DEDICATED

WITH MUCH ADMIRATION FOR HIS FORCE OF CHARACTER AND VERSATILITY OF GENIUS,

BY

HIS OLD SCHOOLFELLOW AND OBLIGED FRIEND,

The Author.

CONTENTS.

PREFACE.

In the first page of the work here reprinted the reader will find these remarkable words, "The Prophet of God, (on whom be His blessing and peace), said: 'Learn the laws of inheritance, and teach them to the people; for they are one half of useful knowledge.'" In truth, the rules of succession must necessarily assume, in countries where the power of testamentary disposition is limited, an importance altogether out of proportion to that which they have with us. Accordingly we find that decisions on the law of inheritance were delivered from the pulpit, and that the study of its various ramifications was not deemed to be beneath the notice of those who enjoyed the highest reputation as sages and as divines. It seldom happens that people professing the same faith can universally agree as to the interpretation of a given text; and, as the passage of the Koran from which the maxims of Moohummudan inheritance are primarily derived is somewhat loosely written, it is not surprising that the rival sects of Omar and Ali, though both looking to the same original source of light, should have arrived at different conclusions on several branches of so momentous a subject. With the system of the Shia sect, the followers of Ali, we have nothing to do here, for the work before us is an authoritative digest of the rules of succession adopted by the Sunni sect, or disciples of Omar.

We know little or nothing of the man to whose industry and energy we owe the compilation of the Sirajiyyah.

Sir William Jones tells us indeed, in the preface to his translation, that the author was one Shaikh Sirajuddin, a native of Sejavend; but he records neither the date of the sage's birth nor the events of his life. It is well known, however, that his work is considered to be of the highest authority, and we have reason to be grateful to Sir William Jones for having issued a translation of this important text-book, with the guarantee afforded by his great reputation as an Oriental linguist.

Of the Sirajiyyah itself it may be said that it contains definitions and rules which, if thoroughly understood and properly applied, are sufficient to enable us to solve most (perhaps all) of the problems which may occur in actual practice. But, in order to make use of its precepts, it is necessary to study it conscientiously, and to re-arrange its matter in a manner more consonant with European habits of thought. This task I endeavoured to perform in my "Chart of Inheritance, according to Orthodox Moohummudan Law," a work which has been favourably received in England, and which is now obtaining a rapid sale in India.

In the treatise which forms a part of that work, I have classified and tabulated the various subjects, and I have thus enabled the reader to ascertain at a glance, who are the sharers, and what are their several shares; who are residuaries, and who distant kindred; what variations the shares may undergo in particular events; what shares may be taken away by the rules of exclusion; and other points of constant recurrence, which in the Sirajiyyah are found scattered loosely over the pages. In the same work I have pointed out how the most complicated problems may be worked out by European arithmetic, so as to make the reader independent of the interesting but cumbrous methods of the Sirajiyyah, with which few Europeans have had the patience to make themselves acquainted.

The object of the present publication is to supplement my "Chart" with an exact reproduction of the work on which it relies for its authority. It is easy, I believe, for an English lawyer to ascertain what he wants in the "Chart" or its accompanying Treatise, but it would be useless to cite the "Chart" in Court, when "Macnaghten's Principles" would in all probability be cited against it. I am anxious, therefore, to afford practitioners an opportunity of verifying my statements by those of the Sirajiyyah; so that, having found the required definition or rule in the "Chart," they may proceed at once to prove it by reference to the authority.

Let us suppose, for instance, that the deceased has left a father, a wife, and no children. The lawyer will find, in the chapter "Of Sharers" (Chart, p. 8), that the father's share is one-sixth. Turning then to the chapter "Of Residuaries," he will find (Chart, p. 12), that the father is, under the circumstances, a residuary as well as a sharer, so that he will get, in addition to his one-sixth, the residue of the property after payment of the wife's share one-fourth; and will therefore, in the whole, take three-fourths. But we find in Macnaghten (principle 32), that "where there is a son of the deceased, or son's son, how low soever, or two or more brothers and sisters, the father will take one-sixth"; and (note to principle 13), "Grandfathers and fathers with sons, son's sons, &c., are legal sharers, but with daughters only they are residuaries, as well as legal sharers." On this authority it might be argued that the father was not entitled to his share, one-sixth, because there was not a son, &c., and that he was not a residuary, because there were no daughters. Consequently, it would be urged that the father would get nothing! Referring, however, to this reprint, p. 5, we find the statements of the Chart clearly supported by the authority of the Sirajiyyah.

Suppose, again, that a man leaves a daughter, and also a

father's mother's father, and a mother's mother's father. In the "Chart," p. 6, it is shown that these are false grandparents, and as false grandparents are distant kindred, the daughter will take, first her share, one-half, and then the rest of the estate by the return; so that she will, in fact, get all the property. But in Macnaghten's work (principle 42) the only persons mentioned as false grandparents are the maternal grandfather and the mother of a maternal grandfather; so that in the proposed case the grandparents would not appear to be false, and therefore they would be sharers, and would deprive the daughter of a considerable part of the property. Appealing again to the native authority, we find (*infra*, pp. 4, 5), that "a false male ancestor is where a female intervenes in the line of ascent." Consequently, as false grandparents are d. k. (p. 34), as the return takes precedence of the d. k. (p. 3), and as the daughter is a sharer (p. 7) and as such is entitled to the return in the absence of residuaries, (chapter on Return, p. 27, &c.), it is clear that the daughter will take the whole.

Let us next suppose that a man leaves a daughter, and a great-uncle's son's son; (in other words, a second cousin of the deceased, through intermediate male relations). The daughter will take one-half as a sharer; and the other half remains to be disposed of. In the Chart (p. 11) we find that the cousin, as coming within the category of paternal uncles of the father and their sons, h. l. s., is a residuary; consequently he will take the residue. Now in Macnaghten's chapter "on sharers and residuaries" we find nothing to indicate that such a relation is a residuary, and in the enumeration contained in principle 43 and the note there given, the father's uncles and their sons &c. are not included. Nor, on the other hand, are they included in principle 47, which enumerates those cousins who, according to Mr. Macnaghten, are distant kindred. The reader is therefore left entirely in doubt as to the position of the male relation in this case, and, consequently, as to the question whether the daughter will have to be satisfied with her share only, or whether she will also, by the return, take the rest of the estate. This confusion would have been avoided if Mr. Macnaghten had been aware of the maxim (*infra*, p. 12), "now the residuary in his own right is every male, in whose line of relation to the deceased no female enters."

In the "Chart" (p. 11), it is stated that son's sons, how low soever, are residuaries, and (p. 5) that residuaries take all that remains after the sharers are satisfied. Mr. Macnaghten (principle 10) tells us that "sons, sons' sons and their lineal descendants, in how low a degree soever, have no specific share assigned to them: The general rule is that they take all the property after the legal sharers are satisfied, unless there are daughters."

Those who trust to this statement will be led into a complication of error. In the first place, as Macnaghten merely alludes to son's, son's sons, and their descendants, the reader would be led to suppose that the right of taking the residue belonged exclusively to relations of this description. But, in fact, this right belongs to any residuaries who may happen to exist, provided they are not excluded by a nearer relation (*infra*, p. 2).

Again, Mr. Macnaghten's words very distinctly include all descendants of the son or son's son, whether through males or through females. Consequently, if a man were to leave, among other relations, a son's daughter's son, or a son's son's daughter's son, it would be argued that such a person would succeed with all the rights of a residuary. That this is not really the case is clear from the definition of a residuary cited above; and it will be seen, *infra*, p. 33, that such a relation is among the d. k., since "A distant kinsman *is* every relation, who is neither a sharer nor a residuary."

The omission of any satisfactory description of residuaries and distant kindred is one of the most fatal defects in Macnaghten's book. As the return takes effect when there are only sharers and distant kindred, but not when there are residuaries, it is of essential importance, in calculating the ultimate portions of the sharers who may be entitled to the return, to know the exact line of demarcation between the other two classes of successors. The line is very clearly drawn by the author of the Sirajiyyah; and the absence of distinct definitions on this subject would frequently jeopardize, as will be seen from the instances above given, the rights of the nearest relations.

The words "grandfather" and "grandmother," in Mr. Macnaghten's book, "are intended to include all ancestors, in whatever degree of ascent, between whom and the deceased no female intervenes." Now, as far as grandfathers are concerned, this would be an accurate description of the "true," (see *infra*, p. 4; definition of false male ancestor.) As regards grandmothers, however, these words indicate no distinction recognised by Moohummudan lawyers, for a true grandmother is not one "between whom and the deceased no female intervenes," but "one between whom and the deceased no false grandfather intervenes." (*infra*, p. 4.) The consequence is, that in describing the shares, &c., of grandmothers (principles 37—41), Mr. Macnaghten only includes a small portion of those who, as true grandmothers, are really entitled to shares. This will be more readily understood by referring to the Table of grandparents (Chart, p. 6), which is framed upon the principles of the Sirajiyyah.

It is impossible for me, in the limited space of this preface, to give a complete retrospective review of Mr. Macnaghten's book; but I have written enough, I imagine, to convince the most sceptical that it is impossible to feel a reasonable hope of being able, by its aid, to work out any given problem. But this is not all. Mr. Macnaghten introduces an original element of uncertainty, by stating (principle 5) that "debts are claimable before legacies, and legacies (which however cannot exceed one-third of the testator's estate), must be paid before the inheritance is distributed." Here the word "estate" is not defined; and an English reader would naturally suppose that it meant the entire property of the deceased. But in fact we find (Chart, p. 1, *note*, and *infra*, p. 2,) that the legacies are to be discharged "out of a third of what remains after the debts are paid." Thus, even if Mr. Macnaghten had provided the most accurate rules for determining the rights of heirs and distant kindred *inter se*, the lawyer who relied on the "Principles" would still lose his labour, for he would be unable to ascertain how much of the property remained to be distributed.

It is somewhat singular that, with such glaring and fatal defects, Macnaghten's "Principles," published forty-four years ago, should have been looked upon till recently as a book of paramount authority on the law of inheritance. If Mr. (afterwards Sir W. H.) Macnaghten had lived to this day, he would, no doubt, have rewritten his book long ago. Unfortunately he died early; and his book, in the temporary absence of other treatises, acquired, soon after its publication, that exaggerated fame which an unintelligible disquisition on an obscure subject can sometimes command. Even at the present time it is frequently cited both in India and at the Privy Council, though it is not accepted, I am informed, with the blind faith that was once bestowed on it. The system of attaching native law officers to the Courts in India has perhaps appeared to many of our Judges to obviate the necessity of studying so complicated a subject; and consequently this very faulty work has held its ground, notwithstanding a growing suspicion that (as regards the law of

Inheritance) it is of no practical use to the lawyer or the student. The more the study of Indian Law progresses, the more will our English practitioners feel the want of some book which succinctly places the true rules of Inheritance before the reader. It was in the hope of being able, to some extent, to supply this want, that I wrote and published my Moohummudan "Chart," and if that work has hitherto been of service to any body, it will be found doubly useful now that the unimpeachable authority on which it is founded is placed within the reach of the reader. In reproducing Sir William Jones's translation I have added an index and notes, to assist the student in connecting and systematizing his information as he proceeds; and an appendix, in which I have worked out the various problems by the Arabian methods. In some instances I have solved the proposed questions by European Arithmetic also, in order to shew the identity of the results; but I have not deemed it necessary to adopt that plan throughout, as I thought it sufficient to point out the way, and to leave the rest to the intelligence of the reader.

A. R.

ABBREVIATIONS

USED IN THE NOTES, APPENDIX, ETC.

Rums. Ch.—" A Chart of Family Inheritance, according to Orthodox Moohummudan Law. With an Explanatory Treatise." By Almaric Rumsey. London: Amer, 1866.

g. c. m. - Greatest common measure.

h. l. s. - How low soever.

d. k. - - Distant kindred.

l. c. d. - Least common denominator.

AL SIRAJIYYAH.

THE INTRODUCTION.

IN THE NAME OF THE MOST MERCIFUL GOD!

PRAISE *be* to God, the Lord of *all* worlds; the praise of those who gave *Him* thanks! And *His* blessing on the best of created beings, Muhammed, and his excellent family! The Prophet of God, (on whom be His blessing and peace!) said:—"Learn the laws of inheritance, and teach them to the people; for they *are* one half of useful knowledge." Our learned in the law (to whom God be merciful!) say:—"There belong to the property of a person deceased four* successive duties *to be performed by the magis-*

* It will be at once perceived that there is not any distinction here, as there is in the English law, between real and personal property. The whole property, whether moveable or immoveable, is applied in the order given in the text, viz.:—

1. Funeral expenses.
2. Debts.
3. Legacies, which are only valid to the extent of one-third of the property remaining after payment of funeral expences and debts.
4. Distribution under the law of inheritance.

It may be well to mention, incidentally, that the dower of the wife is a debt, and comes, therefore, under the second head; but the reader must consult other works (as, for instance, the Hedaya), if he requires special information on the subject of dower, for the

trate: first, his funeral ceremony and burial without superfluity of expence, yet without deficiency; next, the discharge of his just debts from the whole of his remaining effects; then, the payment of his legacies out of a third of what remains after his debts *are* paid; and, lastly, the distribution of the residue among his successors, according to the Divine Book, to the Traditions, and to the Assent of the Learned."* They begin with the persons entitled to shares, who are such as have each a specifick share allotted to them in the book of Almighty God; then they proceed to the residuary heirs by relation, and they are all such as take what remains of the inheritance, after those who are entitled to shares; and, if there be only residuaries, they take the whole pro-

author of the Sirajiyyah, after giving this preliminary statement as to the duties of the magistrate in dividing the property of a deceased person, applies himself, throughout the rest of the book, solely to expounding the rules of distribution under the law of inheritance, which only take effect on that portion of the property which remains after the funeral expences, debts, and legacies, are satisfied. It must be understood that whenever, in subsequent notes, we make use of the word estate, we mean the estate subject to these prior charges.

* The law of inheritance is assumed to be founded on certain passages of the Koran, which are not by any means sufficiently definite to solve the numerous problems which arise in actual practice. The author of the Sirajiyyah was evidently aware of this, for he prudently qualified his reference to "the divine book" with the admission that recourse must be had also to "the traditions," and "the assent of the learned." Without such later interpretations the law of inheritance would have been a source of perpetual contention, instead of being, as it really is at the present day, a fixed, scientific, and beautifully harmonious system.

perty: next to residuaries for special cause, as the master of an enfranchised slave and his *male* residuary heirs; then they return to those entitled to shares according to their respective rights of consanguinity; then to the more distant kindred; then to the successor by contract; then to him who was acknowledged as a kinsman through another, so as not to prove his consanguinity, provided the deceased persisted in that acknowledgment even till he died; then to the person, to whom the whole property was left by will; and lastly to the publick treasury.*

ON IMPEDIMENTS TO SUCCESSION.

Impediments to succession *are* four; 1, Servitude, whether it be perfect or imperfect; 2, Homicide, whether punishable by retaliation, or expiable; 3, Difference of religion; and 4, Difference of country, either actual, as between an alien enemy and an alien

* Of the many classes of people here mentioned we shall be principally concerned with those who inherit by relationship to, or marriage with, the deceased; viz., sharers, residuaries, and distant kindred. In the subsequent pages the reader will find these classes described, and their respective rights defined. It will be sufficient here to ask the reader to remember that sharers are persons who take a definite fraction, e. g., one fourth, one third, or the like; residuaries, those who take the residue after the sharers are satisfied, or the whole if there are no sharers, but can take nothing until the shares have been deducted; distant kindred, those who get the property if there are no sharers or residuaries, but can take nothing if any sharers or residuaries exist. Possibly these general definitions may admit of some exceptions, but it is not necessary to mention such exceptions in this place.

tributary; or qualified, as between a fugitive and a tributary, or between two fugitive enemies from two different states: now a state differs from another by having different forces and sovereigns, there being no community of protection between them.

ON THE DOCTRINE OF SHARES, AND THE PERSONS ENTITLED TO THEM.

The *furud*,* or shares, appointed in the book of Almighty God, are six: a moiety, a quarter, an eighth, two thirds, one third, and a sixth, *some formed* by doubling, and *some* by halving. Now those entitled to these shares are twelve persons; four males, who are the father and the true grandfather or other male ancestor, how high soever *in the paternal line*, the brother by the same mother, and the husband; and eight females, who are the wife, and the daughter, and the son's daughter, or other female descendant how low soever, the sister by one father and mother, the sister by the father's side, and the sister by the mother's side, the mother, and the true grandmother, that is, she who is related to the deceased without the intervention of a false grandfather. (A false male ancestor is, where a female

* The various relations who come within the class of sharers are here enumerated, but it will be found, as we proceed, that the shares are in some cases subject to variation according to particular circumstances, and that relations who are primarily sharers may sometimes be residuaries also or residuaries only.

ancestor intervenes in the line of ascent*). The father takes in three cases; 1, An absolute share, which is a sixth, and that with the son, or son's son, how low soever; 2, A legal share, and a residuary portion also, and that with a daughter, or a son's daughter, how low soever in the degree of descent; 3. He has a simple residuary title, on failure of children and son's children, or other low descendants.†

* "True grandfather" or "true male ancestor," is thus seen to be a male ancestor without any intervening female ancestor. It follows that a true grandfather can only be found in one line of ascent, in other words, he must be a direct male ancestor of the father, or, as it is sometimes expressed, "father's father, how high soever." "True grandmother," or "true female ancestor," on the other hand, is any female ancestor between whom and the deceased no false grandfather intervenes. She may therefore be, (1) an ancestor, in the direct female line, of the mother, (2) an ancestor, in the direct female line, of the father, (3) an ancestor, in the direct female line, of any true grandfather. It follows that, while, on account of the rule of exclusion by an intervening relation (see p. 16), only one true grandfather can inherit, several true grandmothers, on the other hand, can inherit at the same time. The distinction between true and false grandparents is of great importance, because the latter, being distant kindred (see infra, p. 34), cannot inherit if there are any sharers or residuaries. A scheme of true and false grandparents up to five generations will be found in Rums. Ch., p. 7.

† The language in which the father's rights are here defined requires a few words of explanation. He has, first, one-sixth of the estate, of which nothing can deprive him. If there are sons or son's sons, how low soever, they are residuaries, and the father can take nothing more. If there are no sons or son's sons, how low soever, but there are daughters, or daughters of sons or of son's sons, how low soever, these females are sharers, but after payment of their shares and any other shares, such as the wife's or mother's, the father is a residuary, and takes all that remains,

The true grandfather has the same interest with the father, except in four cases, which we will mention presently, if it please God; but the grandfather is excluded by the father, *if he be living;* since the father is the mean of consanguinity between the grandfather and the deceased.* The mother's children also take in three cases: a sixth is the share of one only; a third, of two, or of more: males and females have an equal division and right;† but the mother's children are excluded by children of the deceased and by son's children, how low soever, as well as by the father and the grandfather; as the

in addition to his indefeasible share, one-sixth. The expressions "other low descendants" and "son's daughter, how low soever," must be read with this limitation, that the descendants or daughter so mentioned must be the offspring of a son or son's son, h. l. s., for otherwise they would be d. k. (see p. 34), and could take nothing while any residuaries were in existence. The matter appears rather complicated at first sight, but it may be concisely expressed in the following short formula, which we quote from Rums. Ch., p. 12, "where there are sons h. l. s., the father takes only his share, one sixth, and when there are none he is a residuary also."

* The true grandfather is excluded if the father or an intermediate true grandfather be living, as will appear from the rules of exclusion (see p. 16); but otherwise he stands, as we see here, in the place of the father, and has the same rights, both as a sharer and as a residuary.

† By "the mother's children" are meant the brothers and sisters by the same mother only. It will be seen from the text that they are sharers, whatever the sex may be, and that they take equally as among themselves, thus showing an exception to the rule which we shall find laid down in so many other cases, giving to a male the portion of two females related in the same degree (see p. 7 &c.). With regard to sisters by the same father only, see p. 10.

learned agree. The husband takes in two cases; half, on failure of children, and son's children, and a fourth, with children or son's children, how low soever they descend.*

ON WOMEN.

Wives take in two cases; a fourth *goes* to one or more on failure of children, and son's children, how low soever; and an eighth with children or son's children, in any degree of descent.† Daughters begotten by the deceased take in three cases: half *goes* to one only, and two thirds to two or more; and, if there be a son, the male has the share of two females, and he makes them residuaries.‡ The son's daughters

* Here, and in some other places, it must be remembered that the children of sons, son's sons, &c., h. l. s., are meant; for daughters' children, sons' daughters' children, &c. (wherever, in short, a female intervenes in the descent), are d. k. (see p. 34), and can only become entitled after all sharers are satisfied (see p. 3).

† The observation made in the last preceding note is applicable here also.

‡ That is to say, that if there are both sons and daughters, the daughters instead of being sharers become residuaries; they do not, however, divide the residue equally with the sons, but each of them takes half as much as each of the sons. Thus, if there are two sons and three daughters, the residue will be divided into seven parts, of which each son will take two and each daughter one. A female who thus becomes a residuary in consequence of the existence of a particular male relation is called a residuary "in the right of" or "by" another (see p. 14). It will be seen, hereafter, that a similar change may take place with respect to some other female sharers when there are males related to the deceased in the same degree with them.

are like the daughters begotten by the deceased; and they may be in six cases: half goes to one only, and two thirds to two or more, on failure of daughters begotten by the deceased; with a single daughter of the deceased, they have a sixth, completing, (*with the daughter's half*), two thirds; but, with two daughters of the deceased, they have no share of the inheritance, unless there be, in an equal degree with, or in a lower degree than, them, a boy, who makes them residuaries.* As to the remainder between them, the male has the portion of two females; and all of the son's daughters are excluded by the son himself.†

If a man leave three son's daughters, some of them in lower degrees than others, and three daughters of the son of another son, some of them in lower degrees than others, and three daughters of the son's son of another son, some of them in lower degrees than others, as in the following table, this is called the case of *tashbib.*

* Thus, if there be two daughters, one son's daughter, and one son's son (but no son), the two daughters take two thirds between them and thus exhaust the daughter's share, so that the son's daughter takes nothing as a sharer; but the son's son takes two thirds, instead of the whole, of the residue, and the son's daughter takes the remaining one third. It appears, from the illustration which follows, that the same principle applies to lower stages of descent.

† This must be taken to mean, by *any* son, even if not the father of the son's daughters, for otherwise the son's daughters would receive daughters' shares. They would thus be in a more favourable position than daughters (who would be made residuaries by the son) or son's sons (who would be excluded by him).

FIRST SET.	SECOND SET.	THIRD SET.
Son	Son	Son
Son, daughter	Son	Son
Son, daughter	Son, daughter	Son
Son, daughter	Son, daughter	Son, daughter
	Son, daughter	Son, daughter
		Son, daughter.

Here the eldest of the first line has none equal in degree with her; the middle one of the first line is equalled in degree by the eldest of the second; and the youngest of the first line is equalled by the middle one of the second, and by the eldest of the third line; the youngest of the second line is equalled by the middle one of the third line, and the youngest of the third set has no equal in degree.—When thou hast comprehended this, then we say: the eldest of the first line has a moiety; the middle one of the first line has a sixth together with her equal in degree to make up two thirds; and those in lower degrees never take anything, unless there be a son with them, who makes them residuaries, both her who is equal to him in degree, and her who is above him; but who is not entitled to a share: those below him are excluded.

Sisters by the same father and mother may be in five cases: half goes to one alone; two thirds to two or more; and, if there be brothers by the same father and mother, the male has the portion of two females; and the females become residuaries through him by reason of their equality in the degree of relation to the deceased; and they take the residue, when they are with daughters or with son's daughters, by the saying of Him, on whom be blessing and peace! "Make sisters, with daughters, residuaries."*

Sisters by the same father only are like sisters by the same father and mother, and may be in seven cases: half goes to one, and two thirds to two or more on failure of sisters by the same father and mother; and, with one sister by the same father and mother, they have a sixth, as the complement of two thirds; but they have no inheritance with two sisters by the same father and mother,† unless there be with them a brother by the same father, who makes them residuaries; and then the residue is *distributed*

* The position of sisters when there are brothers also will be understood from what has been laid down earlier as to daughters when there are sons also (see p. 7). When there are sisters and daughters or sons' daughters, it is seen, from the text in this place, that instead of the daughters or sons' daughters taking their shares and excluding the sisters, the sisters and the daughters or sons' daughters become residuaries together, and divide the residue equally among them. A female who thus, instead of being excluded, becomes a residuary by reason of the existence of a particular female more nearly related to the deceased, a residuary "with" another (see p. 14).

† If there are several sisters by the same father and mother, as we have seen (see p. 9), they take two thirds, and it is seen here that the sisters' portion is then considered to be exhausted; but if there be only one sister by the same father and mother her share is only a half (see *ibid*), and it is here laid down that one sixth, the difference between one half and two thirds, is to go to the sisters by the same father only. The reader will perceive that these rules are analogous to those laid down with respect to daughters and sons' daughters (see p. 8).

among them *by the sacred rule* "to the male what is equal to the share of two females." The sixth case is, where they are residuaries with daughters or with son's daughters, as we have before stated *it.**

Brothers and sisters by the same father and mother, and by the same father only, are all excluded by the son and the son's son, in how low a degree soever, and by the father *also*, as it is agreed *among the learned*, and even by the grandfather according to Abu Hanifah, on whom be the mercy of Almighty God! And those of the half blood are also excluded by the brothers of the whole blood.

The mother takes in three cases: a sixth with a child, or a son's child, even in the lowest degree, or with two brothers and sisters or more, by whichever side they are related; and a third of the whole on failure of those just mentioned; and a third of the residue after the share of the husband or wife; and this in two cases, either when there are the husband and both parents, or the wife and both parents: if there be a grandfather instead of a father, then the mother takes a third of the whole property, though not by the opinion of Abu Yusuf, on whom be God's mercy! for he says, that in this case also she has only a third of the residue. The grandmother has a sixth, whether she be by the father or by the mother, whether alone or with more, if they be true grandmothers

* It is seen here, that, in the absence of sisters by the same father and mother, the rules as to sisters by the same father are the same (*mutatis mutandis*) as those laid down respecting sisters by the same father and mother (see p. 9). With regard to sisters (and brothers) by the same mother only, see p. 6.

and equal in degree; but they are all excluded by the mother, and the paternal female ancestors also by the father; and, in like manner, by the grandfather, except the father's mother, even in the highest degree; for she takes with the grandfather, since she is not *related* through him. The nearest grandmother, *or female ancestor*, on either side, excludes the more distant grandmother, on whichever side she be; whether the nearer grandmother be entitled to a share of the inheritance, or be herself excluded. When a grandmother has but one relation, as the father's mother's mother, and another has two such relations, or more, as the mother's mother's mother, who is also the father's father's mother, according to this table,

Mother		Mother
Mother	Father	Mother
Father		Mother

then a sixth is divided between them, according to Abu Yusuf, in moieties, respect being had to their persons; but, according to Muhammed, (on whom be God's mercy!) in thirds, respect being had to the sides.

ON RESIDUARIES.

Residuaries by relation *to the deceased* are three: the residuary in his own right, the residuary in another's right, and the residuary together with another.* Now the residuary in his own right is

* It will be readily understood that the first class of residuaries here mentioned consists of male relations of the deceased. These

every male, in whose line of relation to the deceased no female enters; and of this sort there are four classes; the offspring of the deceased, and his root, and the offspring of his father and of his nearest grandfather, a preference being given, I mean a preference in the right of inheritance, according to proximity of degree. The offspring of the deceased are his sons *first;* then their sons, in how low a degree soever: then *comes* his root, or his father; then his paternal grandfather, and their paternal grandfathers, how high soever; then the offspring of his father, or his brothers; then their sons, how low soever; and then the offspring of his grandfather, or his uncles: then their sons, how low soever. Then the strength of consanguinity prevails: I mean, he, who has two relations is preferable to him, who has only one relation, whether it be male or female, according to the saying of Him, on whom be peace! "Surely, kinsmen by the same father and mother shall inherit before kinsmen by the same father only:" thus a brother by the same father and mother is preferred to a brother by the father only, and a sister by the same father and mother, if she become a residuary with the daughter, is preferred to a brother by the father only; and the son of a brother by the same father and mother is preferred to the son of a

(except the father and true grandfather) can never be sharers. Instances of the other two classes (females who become residuaries) will be found above (see pp. 7 &c.). An enumeration of male residuaries, and a statement of the conditions under which the father, true grandfather, and particular females may become residuaries, will be found in Rums. Ch., chap. iv.

brother by the same father only; and the rule is the same in regard to the paternal uncles of the deceased; and, after them, to the paternal uncles of his father, and, after them, to the paternal uncles of his grandfather.

The residuaries in another's right are four females; namely, those whose shares are half and two thirds, and who become residuaries in right of their brothers, as we have before mentioned in their different cases; but she, who has no share among females, and whose brother is the heir, doth not become a residuary in his right; as in the case of a paternal uncle and a paternal aunt.

As to residuaries together with others: such is every female who becomes a residuary with another female; as a sister with a daughter, as we have mentioned before. The last residuary is the master of a freedman, and then his residuary heirs, in the order before stated; according to the saying of Him, on whom be blessing and peace! "the master bears a relation like that of consanguinity;" but females have nothing among the heirs of a manumittor, according to the saying of Him, on whom be blessing and peace!" Women have nothing from their relation to freedmen, except when they have themselves manumitted a slave; or their freedman has manumitted one, or they have sold a manumission to a slave, or their vendee has sold it to his slave, or they have promised manumission after their death, or their promisee has promised it after his death, or unless their freedman or freedman's freedman draw a relation *to them.*"

If the freedman leave the father and son of his manumittor, then a sixth of the right over the property of the freedman vests in the father, and the residue in the son, according to Abu Yusuf; but, according to both Abu Hanifah and Muhammed, the whole right vests in the son; and, if a son and a grandfather of the manumittor be left, the whole right over the freedman goes to the son, as all the learned agree. When a man possesses as his slave a kinsman in a prohibited degree, he manumits him, and his right vests in him; as if there be three daughters, the youngest of whom has twenty *dinars*, and the eldest, thirty; and they two buy their father for fifty *dinars;* and afterwards their father die leaving some property; then two thirds of it are divided in thirds among them, as their legal shares, and the residue goes in fifths to the two who bought their father; three fifths to the eldest and two fifths to the youngest; which may be settled by dividing the whole into forty-five parts.

ON EXCLUSION.

Exclusion is of two sorts: 1. *Imperfect*, or an exclusion from one share, and an admission to another; and this takes place in respect of five persons, the husband or wife, the mother, the son's daughter, and the sister by the same father; and an explanation of it has preceded. 2. *Perfect* exclusion: there are two sets of persons having a claim to the inheritance: one of which sets is not excluded entirely in any case; and they are six persons, the son, the father, the husband, the daughter, the mother, and the wife;

but the other set inherit in one case and in another case are excluded. This is grounded on two principles; one of which is, that "whoever is related to the deceased through any person, shall not inherit, while that person is living;" as a son's son, with the son; except the mother's children, for they inherit with her; since she has no title to the whole inheritance: the second *principle* is, "that the nearest *of blood* must take," and who the nearest is, we have explained *in the chapter* on residuaries. A person incapable of inheriting doth not exclude any one, *at least* in our opinion; but, according to Ibnu Masuud (may God be gracious to him!) he excludes imperfectly; as an infidel, a murderer, and a slave. A person excluded may, as all *the learned* agree, exclude *others*; as, *if there be* two brothers or sisters or more, on whichever side they are, they do not inherit with the father *of the deceased*, yet they drive the mother from a third to a sixth.*

* This chapter will probably seem to the reader to be rather meagre, for it does not give, as might be expected, an enumeration of the persons who exclude and the persons who are excluded by them. On the other hand it may also appear somewhat illogical, as it gives the case of a mother who is "driven," under certain circumstances, from one third to one sixth, as a case of exclusion. In answer to the objection first suggested, it may be observed that the principal cases of exclusion, though scattered about the book, will be found without much trouble; the circumstances under which a particular relation is excluded being generally mentioned by the author when he is treating of the share of that relation. The peculiar use of the word "exclusion" probably arises from the translator having been unable to find an exact equivalent for the word used in the original. In Rums. Ch., chap. ix., where the word "exclusion" is used in the natural sense of *total* exclusion, a table of the principal instances of such

ON THE DIVISORS OF SHARES.

Know, that the six shares mentioned in the book of Almighty God are of two sorts:* of the first are a moiety, a fourth, and an eighth; and of the second sort are two thirds, a third, and a sixth, as the fractions are halved and doubled. Now, when any of these shares occur in cases singly, the divisor for each share is that number which gives it its name,† (except half, which is from two) as a fourth denominated from four, an eighth from eight, and a third from three: when they occur by two or three, and are of the same sort, then each integral number is the proper divisor to produce its fraction, and also to produce the double of that fraction, and the double of that, as six produces a sixth, and likewise a third, and two thirds; but, when half, *which is* from the first sort, is mixed with all of the second sort or with some of them, then *the division of the estate must be* by six; when a fourth is mixed with all of the second *sort* or with some of them, then the division must be into twelve; and when an eighth is mixed with all of the

exclusion will be found; while the most important cases of what may be called *partial* exclusion, that is, the substitution of a smaller for a larger share, or the transformation of a sharer into a residuary, will be found enumerated in Rums. Ch., chaps. iii. iv.

* The "first sort," it will be seen, arise when the estate is divided only by two, or powers of two; the "second sort," when the factor three enters into the division.

† For instance, if there is a true grandmother, who takes one sixth, the estate is divided by six, the number which "gives its name" to the share one sixth.

second sort, or with some of them, then it must be into four and twenty parts.*

ON THE INCREASE.

Aul, or *increase*, is, when some fraction remains above the *regular* divisor, or when the divisor is too small to admit one share. Know, that the whole number of divisors is seven, four of which have no increase, namely, two, three, four, and eight; and three of them have an increase. The *divisor*, six, is, therefore, increased by the *aul* to ten, either by odd, or by even, numbers; twelve is raised to seventeen by odd, not by even, numbers; and twenty-four is raised to twenty-seven by one increase only; as in the case, called *Mimberiyya*, (or a case answered by Ali when he was in the pulpit) which was this, "*A man left* a wife, two daughters, and both his parents." After

* Thus, if there be a daughter, who takes one half, and a wife, who (as there is a child) takes one eighth, the estate must be divided by eight; if there be several daughters, who take two thirds, and a mother who (as there are children) takes one sixth, it must be divided by six; if there be several daughters, who take two thirds, and a husband, who (as there are children) takes one fourth, it must be divided by twelve; if there be several daughters, who take two thirds, and a wife, who (as there are children) takes one eighth, it must be divided by twenty-four. It will be easily perceived that these rules are constructed for the purpose of enabling the native lawyer, without going through any scientific process, to assign immediately what is called in European arithmetic the "least common denominator" of any set of fractions that may occur together. It may be as well to mention here that the divisor is frequently called the "root" in subsequent parts of the work.

this there can be no increase, except according to Ibn Masuud, (may God be gracious to him!) for, in his opinion, the divisor twenty-four may be raised to thirty-one; as *if a man leave* a wife, his mother, two sisters by the same parents, two sisters by the same mother only, and a son rendered incapable of inheriting.*

ON THE EQUALITY, PROPORTION, AGREEMENT, AND DIFFERENCE OF TWO NUMBERS.

The temathul of two numbers in† the equality of one to the other; the *tedakhul* is, when the smaller of two numbers exactly measures the larger, or exhausts

* The process here described is not an augmentation of the shares, as the name given to it would most naturally suggest, but, on the contrary, a proportionate diminution of the shares when they cannot be paid in full, in consequence of the specific fractions, when added together, being greater than unity or the whole. For instance, let there be a husband, a father, a mother, and a daughter, who respectively take one fourth, one sixth, one sixth, and one half. The divisor is twelve, and it is clear that (if possible) the shares should be respectively three twelfths, two twelfths, two twelfths, and six twelfths, or that they would make in all thirteen twelfths. It is obvious that these shares cannot be paid in full; but by the process of the increase the divisor must be increased to thirteen, and the claimants will take respectively three thirteenths, two thirteenths, two thirteenths, and six thirteenths, so that the estate will be exactly divided among the shares in the required ratio of four, two, two, and six. The rule may be simply stated thus:—when the sum of the portions of the claimants is greater than the divisor, the divisor must be increased so as to be equal to that sum.

† This is clearly a misprint for *is*.

it; or we call it *tedakhul*, when the larger of the two numbers is divided exactly by the smaller; or we may define it thus, when the larger exceeds the smaller by one number or more equal to it, or equal to the larger;* or it is, when the smaller is an aliquot part of the larger, as three of nine. The *tawafuk*, or agreement, of two numbers is, where the smaller does not exactly measure the larger, but a third number measures them both, as eight and twenty, each of which is measured by four, and they agree in a fourth;† since the number measuring them is the denominator of a fraction common to both. The *tabayun* of two numbers is, when no third number whatever measures the two discordant numbers, as nine and ten. Now the way of knowing the agreement or disagreement‡ between two different quan-

* It may be conjectured from this passage that the author of the Sirajiyyah was not acquainted with any rule of division such as that which is familiar to European arithmeticians, and that he ascertained the *tedakhul* of numbers by subtraction. This conjecture derives additional force from the fact that, in his rule for finding the agreement (*i. e.* the greatest common measure) of two numbers, he relies upon successive subtraction instead of division, (see p. 21).

† We shall have occasion, in our arithmetical explanations, to use this form of expression very frequently, and it may therefore be as well to mention, once for all, that when any two numbers are said to agree in a fourth, a third, &c. (or in four, three, &c., for that shorter mode of expression is used in the same sense), the meaning is that the last mentioned number is the greatest common measure of the other two. Thus, by the expression, thirty-six and twenty-four agree in a twelfth, or in twelve, we mean that twelve is the greatest common measure of thirty six and twenty-four.

‡ See Appendix, A.

tities is, that the greater be diminished by the smaller quantity on both sides, once or oftener, until they agree in one point; and if they agree in unit only, there is no numerical agreement between them; but, if they agree in any number, then they are (*said to be*) *mutawafik* in a fraction, of which that number is the denominator; if two, in half; if three, in a third; if four, in a quarter; and so on, as far as ten; and, above ten, they agree in a fraction; I mean, if the number be eleven, the fraction of eleven, and, if it be fifteen, by the fraction of fifteen. Pay attention to this *rule*.

ON ARRANGEMENT.

In arranging* cases there is need of seven principles;

* The translator, as he informs us in his Preface, used "arrangement" in the place of an Arabic word for which he was unable to find an exact equivalent. The Eastern order of thought is, indeed, so widely different from ours, that there is no technical term of European arithmetic which could be used singly to designate the process described as "arrangement." The meaning of the word, however, is not obscure or difficult to apprehend. It will be remembered that rules for finding the numbers by which the estate must be divided when several shares have to be assigned to different people were given above, (see p. 17). But at that early stage it was not supposed that there might be more than one claimant for each share, whereas in practice there may be many; as for instance, five sisters taking two thirds between them, two wives taking one eighth between them, and the like. Under the simple circumstances first alluded to, the rules amounted in fact to an enumeration of all the least common denominators that could occur under various circumstances, and the least common denominators at that stage were called divisors, or roots; but

three, between the shares and the persons, and four between persons and persons. Of the three *principles* the first* is, that, if the portions of all the classes be divided among them without a fraction, there is no need of multiplication, as *if a man leave* both parents and two daughters. The second† is, that, if the portions of one class be fractional, yet there be an agreement between their portions and their persons, then the measure of the number of persons, whose shares are broken, must be multiplied by the root of the case, and its increase, it‡ it be an increased case, as, *if a man leave* both parents and ten daughters, or *a woman leave* a husband, both parents, and six daughters. The third§ *principle* is, that, if their portions leave a fraction, and there be no agreement between those portions and the persons, then the whole number of the persons, whose shares are broken, must be multiplied into the root of the case, as *if a woman leave* her husband and five sisters by

such an enumeration is not possible where there are several claimants, as the circumstances are subject to indefinite variation. It is the practice, however, to find the divisor first, as if there were only one claimant for each share, and the "principles of arrangement" are rules for ascertaining what number we must multiply into the divisor in order to calculate the ultimate least common denominator. The word "arrangement" is used indifferently to designate the ultimate least common denominator, or the process by which the multiplier is found. It need hardly be said that in a case of increase (see p. 18), the increased root must be multiplied instead of the original root.

* See Appendix, B.

† See Appendix, C.

‡ This is clearly a misprint for "if."

§ See Appendix, D.

the same father and mother. Of the four *other principles* the first* is, that, when there is a fractional division between two classes or more, but an equality between the numbers of the persons, then the rule is, that one of the numbers be multiplied into the root of the case; as if *there be* six daughters, and three grandmothers, and three paternal uncles. The second† is, when some of the numbers equally measure the others; then the rule is, that the greater number be multiplied into the root of the case; as, *if a man leave* four wives and three grandmothers and twelve paternal uncles. The third‡ is, when some of the numbers are *mutawafik*, or composit, with others; then the rule is, that the measure of the first of the numbers be multiplied into the whole of the second, and the product into the measure of the third, if the product of§ the third be *mutawafik*, or, if not, into the whole of the third, and then into the fourth, and so on, in the same manner; after which the product must be multiplied into the root of the case; as, *if a man leave* four wives, eighteen daughters, fifteen female ancestors, and six paternal uncles. The fourth‖ *principle* is, when the numbers are *mutabayan*, or not agreeing one with another; and then the rule is, that the first of the numbers be multiplied into the whole of the second, and the product multiplied by the whole of the third, and that product into

* See Appendix, E.

† See Appendix, F.

‡ See Appendix, G.

§ This is evidently a misprint for "and."

‖ See Appendix, H.

the whole of the fourth, and the last product into the root of the case; as, *if a man leave* two wives, six female ancestors, ten daughters, and seven paternal uncles.*

SECTION.

When thou desirest to know the share of each class by arrangement,† multiply what each class has from the root of the case by what thou hast already multiplied into the root of the case, and the product is the share of that class; and, if thou desirest to know the share of each individual in that class by arrangement,‡ divide what each class has from the principle

* See Appendix, I.

† We have already been furnished with complete rules for finding the arrangement, or ultimate l. c. d. The author now gives us a rule for finding "the share of each class by arrangement," that is, the number of parts that each class will take out of the entire number into which the estate is divided. In European arithmetical phraseology, having found the l. c. d., we have now to find the numerators of the fractions which represent the portions accruing to the several classes respectively. An example of this rule is worked out, Appendix, J.

‡ Having found the "share of each class by arrangement," we have now to divide that share or portion among the several individuals of the class. For instance, four wives taking five hundred and fifty parts, eighteen daughters taking two thousand eight hundred and eighty parts, &c., we are now taught to calculate the number of parts which each wife, daughter, &c., will take. In other words, having found the numerator for each class, we have now to find the numerator for each individual. For an example (in continuation of that referred to in the last preceding note), see Appendix, K.

of the case by the number of the persons in it, then multiply the quotient into the multiplicand, and the product *will be* the share of each individual in that class. Another method is to divide the multiplied number by whichever class thou thinkest proper, then to multiply the quotient into the share of that set, by which thou hast divided the multiplied number, and the product *will be* the share of each individual in that set. Another method is by the way of proportion, which is the clearest; and it is, that a proportion be ascertained for the share of each class from the root of the case to the number of persons one by one, and that, according to such proportion from the multiplied *number*, a share be given to each individual of that class.

ON THE DIVISION OF THE PROPERTY LEFT AMONG HEIRS AND AMONG CREDITORS.

If there be a disagreement between the property left and the *number arising from the* arrangement, then multiply the portion of each heir, according to that arrangement, into the aggregate of the property, and divide the product of the number of the arrangement, but, when there is an agreement between the arrangement and the property left, then multiply the portion of each heir, according to the arrangement into the measure of the property, and divide the product by the measure of the *number arising from the* arrangement; the quotient is the portion of that heir in both methods. This *rule* is in order to know the portion of each individual among the heirs; but, in order to know the portion of each class of them, multiply what each class has, according to the root of the case, into the measure of the property left, then divide the product by the measure of the case, if there be an agreement between the property left and the case; but, if there be a disagreement between them, then multiply into the whole of the property left, and divide the product by the whole *number arising from the* verification of the case; and the quotient *will be* the portion of that class in both methods.* Now, as to the payment of debts, the debts of all the creditors stand in the place of the arranging number.†

ON SUBTRACTION.

When any one agrees to take a part of the property left, subtract his share from *the number arising* by the proof, and divide the remainder of the property by the portions of those who remain; as, *if a woman leave* her husband, her mother, and a paternal

* The preceding portion of this chapter relates to the division of the actual sum of money (as, so many gold mohurs or the like) among the claimants, when their proportionate shares of the estate are ascertained. The reader will probably, from the previous explanations, be able to understand this part of the work; and, as the problems which arise involve mere questions of arithmetic, not essentially connected with the law of inheritance, we do not think it necessary to offer any examples. The word "*verification*," as we learn from Sir William Jones's preface, is used by him in the same sense as "arrangement."

† See Appendix, L.

uncle: Now *suppose that* the husband agrees to take what was in his power of his bridal gift to the wife; this is deducted from among *the heirs:* then what remains is divided between the mother and the uncle in thirds, according to their legal shares; and thus there will be two parts for the mother, and one for the uncle.*

ON THE RETURN.

The return is the converse of the increase; and it *takes place* in what remains above the shares of those entitled to them, when there is no legal claimant of it: this *surplus* is returned to the sharers according to their rights,† except the husband or the wife; and this is the opinion of all the *Prophet*'s companions, as Ali and his followers, may God be gracious to them! And our masters (to whom God be merciful!) have assented to it: Zaid, the son of Thabit, says, that the surplus doth not revert, but *goes* to the publick treasury; and to this opinion have assented Urwah and Alzuhri and Malic and Alshafii, may God be merciful to them!

Now the cases on this head are *in* four divisions: the first of them *is*, when there is in the case but one

* See Appendix, M.

† In other words, if there are no residuaries, the sharers (except husband or wife) divide the residue among them *in proportion to their shares;* and the d. k. get nothing. The chapter now under consideration gives accurate rules for dividing the property in due proportion. See Appendix, N.

sort of kinsmen, to whom a return must be made, and none of those who are not entitled to a return: then settle the case according to the number of persons; as, when the deceased has left two daughters, or two sisters, or two female ancestors; settle it, therefore, by two. The second *is*, when there are joined in the case two or three sorts of those, to whom a return must be made, without any of those, to whom there is no return: then settle the case according to their shares; I mean by two, if there be two sixths in the case; or by three, when there are a third and a sixth in it; or by four, when there are a moiety and a sixth in it; or by five, when there are in it two thirds and a sixth, or half and two sixths, or half and a third. The third *is*, when in the first case, there is *any one* to whom no return can be made: then give the share of him or her, to whom there is no return, according to the lowest *denominator*, and if the residue exactly quadrate with the number of persons, who are entitled to a return, *it is* well; as *if there be* a husband and three daughters; but, if they do not agree, then multiply the measure *of the number* of the persons, if there be an agreement between the number of persons and the residue, into the denominator of the shares of those, to whom no return is to be made: as *if there be* a husband, and six daughters; if not, multiply the whole number of the persons into the denominator of the share of those, to whom there is no return; and the product will set the case right. The fourth is, when, in the second case, there are any to whom no return is made: then divide what remains from the denominator of the share of him or them, who have no return, by the case of those, to whom a return must be made, and, if the remainder quadrate, *it is well;* and this *is* in one form; that is, when a fourth *goes* to the wives, and the residue is *distributed* in thirds among those entitled to a return; as *if there be* a wife, and a grandmother, and two sisters by the mother's side: but, if it do not quadrate, then multiply the whole case of those, who are entitled to a return, into the denominator of the share of him or her, who is not entitled to it; and the product will be the denominator of the shares of both classes; as *if there be* four wives, and nine daughters, and six female ancestors: then multiply the shares of those, to whom no return must be made, into the case of those, who are entitled to a return, and the shares of those, to whom a return is to be made, into what remains of the denominator of the share of those, who are not entitled to a return. If there be a fraction in some, adjust the case by the before mentioned principles.

ON THE DIVISION OF THE PATERNAL GRANDFATHER.

Abubecr the Just, (on whom be the grace of God!) and those, who followed him, among the companions *of the Prophet*, say, "The brethren of the whole blood and the brethren by the father's side inherit not with the grandfather:" This is also the decision of Abu Hanifa, (on whom be God's mercy!) and judgements are given conformably to it. Zaid the son of Thabit, indeed, asserts, that they *do* inherit with the grandfather, and of this opinion are both *Abu Yusuf and*

Muhammed, as well as Malic and Alshafii According to Zaid, the son of Thabit (on whom be God's mercy !) the grandfather, with brothers or sisters of the whole blood and by the father's side, takes the best in two cases, from the *mukasamah*, or *division*, and from a third of the whole estate. The meaning of *mukasamah* is, that the grandfather is placed in the division as one of the brethren, and the brethren of the half blood enter into the division with those of the whole blood, to the prejudice of the grandfather; but, when the grandfather has received his allotment, then the half blood are removed from the rest, *as if* disinherited, and receive nothing; and the residue goes to the brethren of the whole blood; except when, among those of the whole blood there is a single sister, who receives her legal share, I mean the whole after the grandfather's allotment: then, if anything remains, *it goes* to the half blood; if not, they have nothing; and this *is the case*, when *a man leaves* a grandfather, a sister by the same father and mother, and two sisters by the same father only: *in this case* there remains to those sisters a tenth of the estate, and the correct denominator *is* twenty; but, if there be, in the preceding case, one sister by the same father only, nothing remains for her; and if one, entitled to a legal share, be mixed with them, then, after he has received his share, the grandfather has the best in the three arrangements; either the division, when *a woman leaves* her husband, a grandfather, and a brother; or a third of the residue *is given*, when a man leaves a grandfather, a grandmother, and two brothers, and a sister by the same father and mother. Or a sixth of the whole estate *is given*, when a man leaves a grandfather and a grandmother, a daughter, and two brothers; and, when a third of the residue is better from the grandfather, and the residue has not a complete third, multiply the denominator of the third into the root of the case. If a woman leave a grandfather, her husband, a daughter, her mother, and a sister by the same father and mother, or by the same father only, then a sixth is best for the grandfather, and the *root of the* case is raised to thirteen, and the sister has nothing. Know, that Zaid, the son of Thabit (on whom be God's grace!) has not placed the sister by the same father and mother, or by the same father, as entitled to a share with the grandfather, except in the case, named *acdariyyah*, and that is, the husband, the mother, a grandfather, and a sister by the same father and mother, or by the same father only; *in which case* the husband *ought to have* a moiety; the mother, a third; the grandfather, a sixth; and the sister, a moiety; then the grandfather annexes his share to that of the sister, and, a division is made between them *by the rule* "a male has the portion of two females;" *and this is*, because the division is best for the grandfather. The root is *regularly* six, but is increased to nine, and a correct distribution is made by twenty-seven. The case is called *acdariyyah*, because it occurred on *the death of* a woman belonging to the tribe of Acdar. If, instead of the sister, there be a brother or two sisters, there is no increase, nor *is that case* an *acdariyyah*.*

* This disquisition on the rights of a particular relative is of

ON SUCCESSION TO VESTED INTERESTS.

If some of the shares become vested inheritances before the distribution, as *if a woman leave* her husband, a daughter, and her mother, and the husband die, before the estate can be distributed, leaving a wife and both his parents, *if* then the daughter die leaving two sons, a daughter, and a *maternal* grandmother, and then the grandmother die leaving her husband and two brothers, the principle in this *event* is, that the case of the first deceased be arranged, and that the allotment of each heir be *considered* as delivered according to that arrangement; that, next, the case of the second deceased be arranged, and that a comparison be made between what was in his hands, *or vested in interest*, from the first arrangement, and between the second arrangement, in three situations; and if, on account of equality, what *is* in his hands from the first arrangement quadrate with the second arrangement, then there is no need of multiplication; but, if it be not right, then see whether there be an agreement between the two, and multiply the measure of the second arrangement into the whole of the first arrangement; and, if there be a disagreement between them, then multiply the whole of the second arrangement into the whole of the first arrangement,

course out of place here, when we are considering the general principles by which the arithmetical division is carried out. We leave it, however, as it stands, in order to adhere strictly to that part of our plan which consists in presenting to the legal profession and the public an exact reproduction of Sir William Jones's translation.

and the product *will be* the denominator of both cases. The allotments of the heirs of the first deceased must be multiplied into the former multiplicand, I mean into the second arrangement or into its measure; and the allotments of the heirs of the second deceased must be multiplied into the whole of what *was* in his hands, or into its measure; and, if a third or a fourth die, put the second product in the place of the first arrangement, and the third case in the place of the second, in working; *and* thus in *the case of* a fourth and a fifth, and so on to infinity. *

ON DISTANT KINDRED.

A distant kinsman *is* every relation, who is neither

* The expression "vested interest" or "vested inheritance" must not be understood in the sense which would seem most natural to English lawyers, namely, a share which vested in the lifetime of the *propositus;* for, as the Moohummudan law does not make provision for any right of representation, no estate or interest of that kind can come into existence. "Vested inheritance," in the language of the Sirajiyyah, means a portion of the estate which has actually accrued by the death of the *propositus* but which has not been separated from the rest of the property, because the estate has not been divided during the lifetime of the person entitled to such portion. When the division is at length effected, some of the surviving heirs of the *propositus* may be heirs also of the person who has so died, and some may not. The chapter now under consideration gives rules for effecting the division of the estate of the *propositus* among all the claimants under such circumstances. The problems which arise in this manner are occasionally very complicated when several of the heirs have died successively before the division of the property. See Appendix, O.

a sharer nor a residuary.* The generality of the *Prophet's* companions repeat a tradition concerning the inheritance of distant kinsmen; and, according to this, our masters and their followers (may God be merciful to them!) have decided; but Zaid, the son of Thabit, (on whom be God's grace!) says: "there is no inheritance for the distant kindred, but the property *undisposed of* is placed in the publick treasury"; and with him agree Malic and Alshafii, on whom be God's mercy! Now these distant kindred *are* of four classes: the first class is descended from the deceased; and they are the daughters' children, and the children of the son's daughters. The second sort *are* they, from whom the deceased descend; and they are the excluded grandfathers and the excluded grandmothers. The third sort are descended from the parents of the deceased; and they *are* the sister's children, and the brother's daughters, and the sons of brothers by the same mother only. The fourth sort are descended from the two grandfathers and two grandmothers of the deceased; and they are, paternal aunts, and uncles by the same mother *only*, and

* This is a clear definition, and it shows that the expression "distant kindred" includes all relations, however remote, who do not come within the definition of "sharer" or "residuary." It is necessary to call attention to this point, as some English writers have entirely overlooked the definition, having been misled, apparently, by the classification which follows, and having imagined that only certain limited classes of relations were included in the d. k. The reader will observe, however, that at the end of the classification the author of the Sirajiyyah adds the words, "these, *and all who are related to the deceased through them*, are among the distant kindred."

maternal uncles and aunts. These, and all who are related to the deceased through them, are among the distant kindred. Abu Sulaiman reports from Muhammed the son of Alhasan, *who reported* from Abu Hanifah (on whom be God's mercy!) that the second sort are the nearest of the *four* sorts, how high soever they ascend; then the first, how low soever they descend; then the third, how low soever; and lastly, the fourth, how distant soever *their degree:* but Abu Yusuf and Alhasan, the son of Ziyad, report from Abu Hanifah, (on whom be the mercy of God!) that the nearest of the *four* sorts is the first, then the second, then the third, then the fourth, like the order of the residuaries; and this *is* taken *as a rule* for decision. According to both *Abu Yusuf and Muhammed*, the third sort has a preference over the maternal grandfather.

ON THE FIRST CLASS.

The best entitled of them to the succession is the nearest of them in degree to the deceased; as the daughter's daughter, who is preferred to the daughter of the son's daughter; and, if *the claimants* are equal in degree, then the child of an heir is preferred to the child of a distant relation;* as the daughter of a

* The reader will observe that the word "heirs" means "sharers or residuaries," and does not include the distant kindred. This may be gathered from many parts of the Sirajiyyah, but it is especially noticeable here, for a distinction is drawn between children of "heirs" and children of other relations. Now it is

son's daughter is preferred to the son of a daughter's daughter; but, if their degrees be equal, and there be

clear, as observed in the last preceding note, that the distant kindred include all relations, however remote, who are not sharers or residuaries; consequently, if the word "heirs" included the distant kindred, there could be no other relations whatever, and the distinction just mentioned would be unmeaning. In the example here given in the text the distinction is exemplified, for we have, on the one hand, as the "child of an heir," a daughter of a son's daughter, and on the other hand, as the "child of a distant relation," a son of a daughter's daughter. The reader will find, on looking back to the chapter "On Women," that a son's daughter is a sharer or a residuary, according to circumstances (see p. 7), while a daughter's daughter is neither a sharer nor a residuary under any circumstances.

The remainder of this chapter, and some portions of the other chapters on d. k., relate to the question, whether males and females related in the same degree, but descended through intermediate relations of different sexes, are to take in the usual manner, *viz.* a double share to the male *per capita*, or whether, on the other hand, the difference of sex is to be considered with reference to the intermediate relations. The general analogy of the law of inheritance, which does not recognise the principle of representation, would seem to favour the former view; but the latter, as will be seen by the concluding sentences of this chapter, is considered by the author of the Sirajiyyah to be more generally accepted. We do not propose to trouble the reader with lengthy explanations on the subject of the d. k., which will be sufficiently understood from the text, if the previous portions of the work have been mastered; but an example illustrative of the particular point above alluded to will be found at Appendix, P. A short summary of the rules of inheritance in the several classes of d. k. will be found in Rums. Ch., chap. v. With regard to the first class of d. k., the special subject of this chapter, the reader will remember that the first class of d. k. "is descended from the deceased" (see p. 34); that is to say, it consists of all descendants of the *propositus* who are not so related to him as to be sharers or residuaries.

not among them the child of an heir, or, if all of them be the children of heirs, then, according to Abu Yusuf (may God be merciful to him!) and Alhasan, son of Ziyad, the persons of the branches are considered, and the property is distributed among them equally, whether the condition of the roots, as male or female, agree or disagree; but Muhammed (on whom be God's mercy!) considers the persons of the branches, if the sex of the roots agree, *in which respect* he concurs with the other two; and he considers the persons of the roots, if their sexes be different, and, he gives to the branches the inheritance of the roots, in opposition to the two *lawyers.* For instance, when *a man* leaves a daughter's son, and a daughter's daughter, *then*, according to Abu Yusuf and Alhasan, the property is distributed between them, *by the rule* "the male has the portion of two females," their persons being considered; and, according to Muhammed, in the same manner; because the sexes of the roots agree: and, if *a man* leave the daughter of a daughter's son, and the son of a daughter's daughter, *then*, according to the two *first mentioned lawyers*, the property *is divided* in thirds between the branches, by considering the persons, two thirds of it *being given* to the male, and one third to the female; but, according to Muhammed, (on whom be God's mercy!) the property *is divided* between the roots, I mean *those* in the second rank, in thirds, two thirds *going* to the daughter of the daughter's son, *namely*, the allotment of her father, and one third of it to the son of the daughter's daughter, *namely*, the share of his mother. Thus, according to

Muhammed, (to whom God be merciful!) when the children of the daughters are different *in sex*, the property is divided according to the first rank *that* differs among the roots; then the males are arranged in one class, and the females in another class, after the division, and what goes to the males is collected and distributed according to the highest difference, that occurs among their children, and, in the same manner, what goes to the females; and thus the operation is continued to the end according to this scheme:

S	S	S	D	D	D	D	D	D	D	D	D
D	D	D	D	D	D	D	D	D	D	D	D
S	D	D	S	S	S	D	D	D	D	D	D
D	D	D	S	D	D	S	S	S	D	D	D
D	S	D	D	D	D	S	D	D	S	D	D
D	D	D	D	D	S	D	D	S	D	S	D

Thus Muhammed (to whom God be merciful!) takes the sex from the root at the time of the distribution, and the number from the branches; as, *if a man* leave two sons of a daughter's daughter's daughter, and a daughter of a daughter's daughter's son, and two daughters of a daughter's son's daughter, in this form:

THE DECEASED.

Daughter	Daughter	Daughter
Son	Daughter	Daughter
Daughter	Son	Daughter
Two daughters	Daughter	Two sons

in this case according to Abu Yusuf (on whom be God's mercy!) the property is divided among the branches in seven parts, by considering their persons; but, according to Muhammed, (to whom God be merciful!) the property is distributed according to the highest difference *of sex*, I mean in the second rank, in sevenths, by the number of branches in the roots; and, according to him, four sevenths of it *go* to the daughters of the daughter's son's daughter; since that is the share of their grandfather, and three sevenths of it, which are the allotment of the two daughters, are divided between their two children, I mean those in the third rank, in moieties; one moiety to the daughter of the daughter's daughter's son, *which* is the share of her father, and the other moiety to the two sons of the daughter's daughter's daughter, *being* the share of their mother: the correct divisor of the property is, in this case, twenty-eight. The opinion of Muhammed (on whom be God's mercy!) is the more generally received of the two traditions from Abu Hanifah (to whom God be merciful!) in all decisions concerning the distant kindred; and this was the first opinion of Abu Yusuf; then he departed *from it*, and said that the roots were by no means to be considered.

A SECTION.

Our learned *lawyers* (on whom be the mercy of God!) consider the *different* sides in succession; except that Abu Yusuf (may God be merciful to him!)

considers the sides in the persons of the branches, and Muhammed, (on whom be God's mercy!) considers the sides in the roots; as, when *a man* leaves two daughters of a daughter's daughter, who *are* also the two daughters of a daughter's son, and the son of a daughter's daughter, according to this scheme;

THE DECEASED.

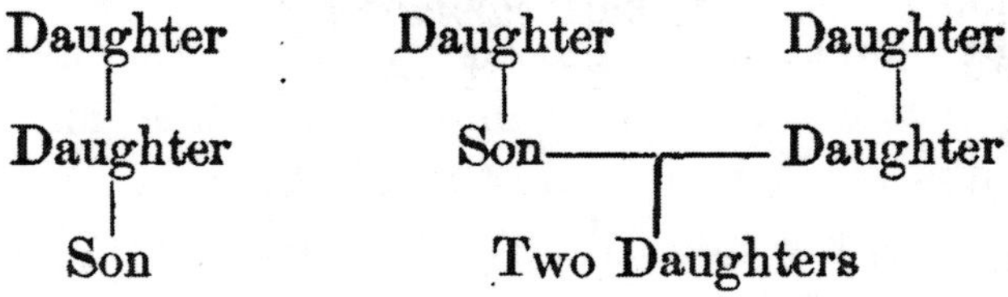

In this case, according to Abu Yusuf, the property *is divided* among them in thirds, and then the deceased is considered as if he had left four daughters and a son; two thirds of it, therefore, go to the two daughters, and one third to the son; but, according to Muhammed (to whom God be merciful!) the estate *is divided* among them in twenty-eight parts, to the two daughters twenty-two shares (sixteen in right of their father and six shares in right of their mother) and to the son six shares in right of his mother.*

* This chapter, entitled "A Section," simply relates to the question before alluded to, whether the advantage of sex should depend on the sex of the actual claimants, or on that of the persons through whom they are descended from the *propositus*. This question is pretty fully treated in the chapters "On the First Class," "On the Second Class," &c.; but it is to be presumed that this additional disquisition was inserted afterwards, in order to emphasize still more clearly the author's views on the subject.

ON THE SECOND CLASS.

He among them, who is preferred in the succession, is the nearest of them to the deceased, on which side soever he stands; and, in the case of equality in the degrees of proximity, then he, who is related to the deceased through an heir, is preferred by the opinion of Abu Suhail, *surnamed* Alferaidi, of Abu Fudail Alkhassaf, and of Ali, the son of Isai Albasri; but, no preference *is given* to him according to Abu Sulaiman Aljurjani, and Abu Ali al Baihathi Albusti. If their degrees be equal, and there be none among them, who is related through an heir, or, if all of them be related through an heir, then, if the sex of those, through whom they are related, agree, and their relation be on the same side, the distribution is according to their persons, but if the sex of those, to whom they are related, be different, the property is distributed according to the first rank that differs in sex, as in the first class; and, if their relation differ, then two thirds *go* to those on the father's side, that *being* the share of the father, and one third *goes* to those on the mother's side, that *being* the share of the mother: then what has been allotted to each set is distributed among them, as if their relation were the same.*

* The second class, it will be remembered, consists of those relations "from whom the deceased descends" (see p. 34); that is to say, all the male and female ancestors of the *propositus*, except those of them who are sharers or residuaries. In other words, the second class consists of false grandfathers and false grandmothers.

ON THE THIRD CLASS.

The rule concerning them is the same with that concerning the first class; I mean, *that* he *is* preferred in the succession, who is nearest to the deceased: and, if they be equal in relation, then the child of a residuary *is* preferred to the child of a more distant kinsman; as, *if a man leave* the daughter of a brother's son, and the son of a sister's daughter, both of them by *the same* father and mother, or by *the same* father, or one of them by *the same* father and mother, and the other by *the same* father *only: in this case* the whole estate *goes* to the daughter of the brother's son, because she is the child of a residuary; and, if it be by *the same* mother *only, distribution is made* between them *by the rule,* "A male has the share of two females," *and*, by the opinion of Abu Yusuf (to whom God be merciful!) in thirds, according to the persons, but, by that of Muhammed, (may God be merciful to him!) in moieties according to the roots; and, if they be equal in proximity, and there be no child of a residuary among them, or *if* all of them be children of residuaries, or if some of them be children of residuaries, and some of them children of those entitled to shares, and their relation differ, then Abu Yusuf (to whom God be merciful!) considers the strongest *in consanguinity;* but Muhammed (may God be merciful to him!) divides the property among the brothers and sisters in moieties, considering as well the number of the branches, as the sides in the roots; and what has been allotted to each set is distributed among their branches, as in the first class: thus, *if a man leave* the daughter of the daughter of a sister by *the same* father and mother, she is preferred to the son of the daughter of a brother by the same father *only*, according to Abu Yusuf (to whom God be merciful!) by reason of the strength of relation; but, according to Muhammed, (may God be merciful to him) the property is divided between them both in moieties by consideration of the roots. So, when *a man* leaves three daughters of different brothers, and three sons and three daughters of different sisters, *as* in this figure:

THE DECEASED.

Sister—Sister—Sister—Brother—Brother—Brother

by the same

Mother—Father—Father—Mother—Father—Father
and Mother *and* Mother

Son Son Son Daughter Daughter Daughter
Daughter Daughter Daughter.

In this case, according to Abu Yusuf, the property is divided among the branches of the whole blood, then among the branches by the same father, then among the branches by the same mother, *according to the rule* "the male has the allotment of two females," in fourths, by considering the persons; but, according to Muhammed (to whom God be merciful!) a third of the estate is divided equally among the branches by the same mother, in thirds, by considering the equality of their roots in the division of the parents, and the remainder among the branches of the whole blood in moieties, by considering in the roots the number of the branches; one half to the daughter of the brother, the portion of the father, and the other between the children of the sister, the male having the allotment of two females, by considering the persons; and *the estate* is correctly divided by nine. If *a man* leave three daughters of different brothers' sons, in this manner:

The Deceased.

Daughter—Daughter—Daughter

Of a Son of a Brother by the same

Father and Mother—Father—Mother

all the property goes to the daughter of the son of the brother by the same father and mother, by the unanimous opinion *of the learned*, since she is the child of a residuary, and hath also the strength of consanguinity.*

ON THE FOURTH CLASS.

The rule as to them *is*, that, when there is only one of them, he has a right to the whole property, since there is none to obstruct him; and, when there are several, and the sides of their relation are the

* The third class "are descended from the parents of the deceased" (see p. 34); that is, they are all descendants of the parents of the *propositus* (other, of course, than those descended from the *propositus* himself), who are not sharers or residuaries.

same, as paternal aunts and paternal uncles by the same mother *with the father*, or maternal uncles and aunts, then the stronger of them in consanguinity is preferred, by the general assent; I mean, they, who are *related* by father and mother, are preferred to those, who are *related* by the father *only*, and they, who are *related* by the father, are preferred to those, who are *related* by the mother only, whether they be males or females; and, if there be males and females and their relation be equal, then the male has the allotment of two females; as, *if there be* a paternal uncle and aunt both by *one* mother, or a maternal uncle and aunt, both by the same father and mother, or by the same father, or by the same mother only: and if the sides of their consanguinity be different, then no regard *is shown* to the strength of relation; as, if *there be* a paternal aunt by the same father and mother, and a maternal aunt by the same mother, or a maternal aunt by the same father and mother, and a paternal aunt by the same mother only, then two thirds *go* to the kindred of the father, for they *are* the father's allotment, and one third to the kindred of the mother, for that *is* the mother's allotment; then what is allotted to each set is divided among them, as if the place of their consanguinity were the same.*

* The fourth class, it will be remembered, are "descendants from the two grandfathers and two grandmothers of the deceased" (see p. 34). The reader will perceive that this class has some special rules of its own, as distinguished from the other classes of d. k.

ON THEIR CHILDREN, AND THE RULES CONCERNING THEM.

The rule as to them *is* like the rule concerning the first class; I mean, *that* the best entitled of them to the succession is the nearest of them to the deceased on which ever side he is *related;* and, if they be equal in relation, and the place of their consanguinity be the same, then he, who has the strength of blood,* is preferred, by the general assent; and, if they be equal in degree and in blood, and the place of their consanguinity be the same, then the child of a residuary *is* preferred to whoever is not *such;* as, *if a man leave* the daughter of a paternal uncle, and the son of a paternal aunt, both of them by *the same* father and mother, or by *the same* father, all the property goes to the daughter of the paternal uncle; and, if one of them be by *the same* father and mother, and the other by the same father only, *then* all the estate goes to the claimant, who has the strength of consanguinity, according to the clearer tradition; *and this* by analogy to the maternal aunt by the same father, for though she be the child of a distant kinsman, yet she is preferred, by the strength of consanguinity, to the maternal aunt by the *same* mother *only*, though she be the child of an heir; since the weight which prevails by itself, that is, the strength of consanguinity, is greater than the weight by another, which is the descent from an heir. Some of them (the

* By the words "the strength of blood," the author means (as the reader will probably have gathered from previous passages), the whole blood as distinguished from the half blood.

learned) say, *that* the whole estate goes to the daughter of the paternal uncle by the same father, since she is the daughter of a residuary; and, if they be equal in degree, yet the place of their relation differ, they have no regard *shown* to the strength of consanguinity, nor to the descent from a residuary, according to the clearer tradition; by analogy to the paternal aunt by the same father and mother, for though she have two bloods, and be the child of an heir on both sides, and her mother be entitled to a legal share, *yet* she is not preferred to the maternal aunt by the *same* father; but two thirds *go* to whoever is related by the father; and there regard is shown to the strength of blood; then to the descent from a residuary; and one third *goes* to whoever is related by the mother, and there *too* regard is shewn to strength of consanguinity: then, according to Abu Yusuf, (may God be merciful to him!) what belongs to each set is divided among the persons of their branches, with attention to the number of sides in the branches; and, according to Muhammed, (may God be merciful to him!) the property is distributed by the first line, *that* differs, with attention to the number of the branches and of the sides in the roots, as in the first class; then this rule is applied to the sides of the paternal uncles of his parents and their maternal uncles; then to their children; then to the side of the paternal uncles of the parents of his parents, and to their maternal uncles; then to their children, as in the *case of* residuaries.

ON HERMAPHRODITES.

To the hermaphrodite, *whose sex is quite* doubtful, *is allotted* the smaller of two shares, I mean the worse of two conditions, according to Abu Hanifah, (may God be merciful to him!) and his friends, and this is the doctrine of the generality of the *Prophet's* companions, (may God be gracious to them!) and conformable to it are decisions *given;* as, when *a man* leaves a son, and a daughter, and an hermaphrodite, then the hermaphrodite has the share of a daughter, since that is ascertained: and according to Aamir Alshabi, (and this is the opinion of Ibnu Abbas, may God be gracious to them both!) the hermaphrodite has a moiety of the two shares in the controversy; but *the two great lawyers* differ in putting in practice the doctrine of Alshabi; *for* Abu Yusuf says, *that* the son has one share, and the daughter half a share, and the hermaphrodite three fourths of a share, since the hermaphrodite would be entitled to a share, if he were a male, and to half a share, if he were a female, and this *is* settled by *his* taking half the sum of the two portions; or, we may say, he takes the moiety which is ascertained, together with half the moiety which is disputed, so that there come to him three fourths of a share; for he (Abu Yusuf) pays attention to the legal share and to the increase, and he verifies *the case* by nine: or, we may say, the son has two shares, and the daughter one share, and the hermaphrodite a moiety of the two allotments, and that *is* a share and half a share. But Muhammed (may God be merciful to him!) says, that the hermaphrodite would take two fifths of the estate, if he were a male, and a fourth of the estate, if he were a female, and that he takes a moiety of the two allotments, and that *will give him* one fifth and an eighth by attention to both sexes; and the case is rectified by forty; since that is the product of one of the *numbers in the* two cases, which is four, multiplied into the other, which is five, and that product multiplied by two (*which is the number of the*) cases; and then he, who takes anything by five, *has it* multiplied into four, and he, who takes anything by four, *has it* multiplied into five; so that thirteen shares *go* to the hermaphrodite, and eighteen to the son, and nine to the daughter.*

ON PREGNANCY.

The longest time of pregnancy *is* two years, accord-

* The word used by the translator as the title of this chapter, (derived, as every classical reader will remember, from one of Ovid's fantastic legends), signifies, in the English language, an individual possessing the essentials of both sexes, a monster which modern research has long since pronounced to be non-existent, or, at any rate, to be unauthenticated by any trustworthy record. But it will be seen from the text (see p. 48) that the Arabic word signifies a person whose sex is "doubtful;" and it was reasonable, at a period when anatomical science must necessarily have been in its infancy, to lay down rules for such cases. At the present time, when surgical knowledge is much more advanced, it is not likely that this chapter can be of any practical use; but it is reprinted with the rest of the book, in order that the reader may have a perfect reproduction of the Sirajiyyah before him.

ing to Abu Hanifah (may God be merciful to him!) and his companions; and according to Laith, the son of Sad Alfahmi, (may God be merciful to him!) three years; and, according to Alshafii, (may God be merciful to him!) four years: but according to Alzuhri, (may God be merciful to him!) seven years: and the shortest time for it is six months.* There is reserved for the child in the womb, according to Abu Hanifah (may God be merciful to him!) the portion of four sons, or the portion of four daughters, whichever of the two is most; and there is given to the rest of the heirs the smallest of the portions; but, according to Muhammed (may God be merciful to him!) there is reserved the portion of three sons or of three daughters, whichever of the two is most: Laith, son of Sad, (may God be gracious to him!) reports this *opinion* from him; but, by another report, *there is reserved* the portion of two sons; and one of the two opinions is that of Abu Yusuf (may God be mer-

* This chapter, like the last preceding, must be considered to belong to a primitive and now discarded system of medical science. It is reprinted, however, for the same reasons that we have assigned for reprinting other apparently useless portions of the work. An English Judge or jury would of course be guided, in any case involving the question of the possible length of pregnancy, by opinions gathered from medical experience, and not by the fanciful notions here recorded, which, in fact, are mere *dicta* of individual jurists, and cannot justly be looked upon as principles of law. The same remarks apply to some of the subsequent portions of this chapter. That part of the chapter, however, which treats of the portion to be reserved for an unborn child, is just and scientific. The rules for calculating this portion will be found *infrà*, pp. 51—53.

ciful to him!) as Hisham reports it from him; but Alkhassaf reports from Abu Yusuf (may God be merciful to him!) that there should be reserved the share of one son or of one daughter; and, according to this, decisions *are made;* and security must be taken, according to his opinion. And, if the pregnancy was by the deceased, and *the widow* produce a child at the full *time* of the longest period *allowed* for pregnancy, or within it, and the woman hath not confessed her having broken her legal term *of abstinence*, *that child* shall inherit, and others may inherit from him; but, if she produce a child after the longest *time* of gestation, he shall not inherit, nor shall others inherit from him: and if the pregnancy was from another man than the deceased, and she, *the kinswoman*, produce a child in six months or less, he shall inherit; but, if she produce the child after the least period of gestation, he shall not inherit.

Now the way of knowing the life of the child at the time of its birth, is, that there be found in him that, by which life is proved; as a voice, or sneezing, or weeping, or smiling, or moving a limb; and, if the smallest *part* of the child come out, and he then die, he shall not inherit; but if the greater *part* of him come out, and then he die, he shall inherit: and, if he come out straight (*or with his head first*) then his breast is considered; I mean, if his whole breast come out, he shall inherit; but if he come out inverted (*or with his feet first*) then his navel is considered.

The chief rule in arranging cases on pregnancy* is,

* See Appendix Q.

that the case be arranged by two suppositions, I mean by supposing, that the child in the womb is a male, and by supposing, that it is a female: then, compare the arrangement of both cases; and, if the numbers agree, multiply the measure of one of the two into the whole of the other; and, if they disagree, then multiply the whole of one of the two into the whole of the other, and the product will be the arranger of the case: then multiply the allotment of him, who would have something from the case, which supposes a male, into that of the case, which supposes a female, or into its measure; and then that of him, who takes on the supposition of a female, into the case of the male, or into its measure, as we have directed concerning the hermaphrodite; then examine the two products of that multiplication; and whether of the two is the less, that shall be given to such an heir; and the difference between them must be reserved from the allotment of that heir; and, when the child appears, if he be entitled to the whole of what has been reserved, it is well; but, if he be entitled to a part, let him take that part, and let the remainder be distributed among the *other* heirs, and let there be given to each of those heirs what was reserved from his allotment: as, when a man has left a daughter and both his parents, and a wife pregnant, then the case *is rectified* by twenty-four on the supposition, that the child in the womb is a male, and by twenty-seven on the supposition, that it is a female: now between the two numbers of the arrangement there is an agreement in a third; and, when the measure of one of the two is multiplied into the whole of the other, the product amounts to two hundred and sixteen, and by that *number* is the case verified; and, on the supposition of its male sex, the wife takes twenty-seven shares, and each of the two parents, thirty-six; but, on the supposition of its female sex, the wife has twenty-four, and each of the parents, thirty-two; and twenty-four are given to the wife, and three shares from her allotment are reserved; and from the allotment of each of the parents are reserved four shares; and thirteen shares are given to the daughter; since the *part* reserved in her right *is* the allotment of four sons, according to Abu Hanifah, (may God be merciful to him!) and when the sons are four, then her allotment is one share and four ninths of a share out of four-and-twenty multiplied into nine, and that makes thirteen shares; and this *belongs* to her, and the residue *is* reserved, which *amounts to* an hundred and fifteen shares. If the widow bring forth one daughter or more, then all the *part* reserved *goes* to the daughters; and, if she bring forth one son or more, then must be given to the widow and both parents what was reserved from their shares; and what remains must be divided among the children: and, if she bring forth a dead child, then must be given to the widow and both parents what was reserved from their shares, and to the daughter a complete moiety, that is, ninety-five shares *more*, and the remainder, which is nine shares, to the father, since he *is* the residuary.

ON A LOST PERSON.

A lost person is *considered as* living in *regard to* his estate; so that no one can inherit from him; and his estate is reserved, until his death can be ascertained; or the term for *a presumption of it* has passed over: now the traditionary opinions differ concerning that term; for, by the clearer tradition, "when, not one of his equals in age remains, judgement may be given of his death;" but Hasan, the son of Ziyad, reports from Abu Hanifah, (may God be merciful to him!) that the term is an hundred and twenty years from the day on which he was born; and Muhammed says, an hundred and ten years; and Abu Yusuf says, an hundred and five years; and some of them, *the learned*, say, ninety years; and according to that *opinion* are decisions *made.* Some of *the learned in the law* say, that the estate of a lost person must be reserved for the final regulation of the *Imam*, and the judgement suspended as to the right of another person, so that his share from the estate of his ancestors must be kept, as in the *case* of pregnancy; and, when the term *is* elapsed, and judgement given of his death, then his estate *goes* to his heirs, *who are* to be found, according to the judgement on his decease; and, what was reserved on his account from the estate of his ancestor, is restored to the heir of his ancestor, from whose estate that share was reserved; since the lost person *is* dead as to the estate of another.

The principle in arranging cases concerning a lost person *is*, that the case be arranged on a supposition of his life, and then arranged on a supposition of his death; and the rest of the operation *is* what we have mentioned in the chapter of pregnancy.*

ON AN APOSTATE.

When an apostate *from the faith* has died naturally, or been killed, or passed into a hostile country, and the *Kadi* has given judgement on his passage *thither*, then what he had acquired at the time of his being a believer, *goes* to his heirs, *who are* believers; and what he has gained since the time of the apostacy

* The opinions here given, as to the length of time which must elapse in order that death may be presumed, are too conflicting to afford any certain rule. This, however, is of little consequence, as the question must reasonably be considered one of fact rather than one of law, except where the special enactments of a particular legislature have established an authoritative rule.

The rule, that anything which would accrue to a lost person is to be reserved, and afterwards, in case of his death being ultimately assumed, divided among the heirs of the ancestor, and not among those of the lost person, is consistent with the well known absence of any right of representation in Moohummudan law. It may, however, have been framed independently of that principle, on the ground that, when the death of a lost person is ultimately assumed, the assumption may relate back to the time of his having become a lost person. The latter theory seems to be favoured by the words in the text, "the lost person is dead as to the estate of another."

With regard to the arithmetical calculations rendered necessary by the reservation of the portions of a lost person and the division of that portion when his death is ultimately assumed, it will not be necessary to enter into any special explanations or to give any examples, as the reader will see from the concluding paragraph of this chapter that these calculations are similar to those previously prescribed for cases of pregnancy (see pp. 51—53).

is placed in the publick treasury, according to Abu Hanifah (may God be merciful to him!) but, according to the two *lawyers* (Abu Yusuf *and* Muhammed) both the acquisitions *go* to his believing heirs; and, according to Alshafii, (may God be merciful to him!) both the acquisitions are placed in the publick treasury; and what he gained after his arrival in the hostile country, that *is* confiscated by the general consent: and all the property of a female apostate *goes* to her heirs, *who are* believers, without diversity of opinion among our masters, to whom God be merciful! but an apostate shall not inherit from any one, neither from a believer nor from an apostate like himself, and so a female apostate shall not inherit from any one; except when the people of a whole district become apostates altogether, for then they inherit reciprocally.

ON A CAPTIVE.

The rule concerning a captive *is* like the rule of other believers in regard to inheritance, as long as he has not departed from the faith; but, if he has departed from the faith, then the rule concerning him *is* the rule concerning an apostate; but, if his apostacy be not known, nor his life nor his death, then the rule concerning him *is* the rule concerning a lost person.*

* See p. 54.

ON PERSONS DROWNED, OR BURNED, OR OVERWHELMED IN RUINS.

When a company *of persons* die, and it is not known which of them died first, they are considered, as if they had died at the same moment; and the estate of each of them *goes* to his heirs, *who are* living; and some of the deceased shall not inherit from others: this is the approved *opinion.* But Ali, and Ibnu Masuud say, according to one of the traditions from them, *that* some of them shall inherit from others, except in what each of them has inherited from the companion of his fate.*

* Suppose, for instance, that the *propositus* has perished by the same calamity with one of his sons, leaving several other sons surviving, and that the deceased son has left children. According to the "approved opinion," the estate of the *propositus* will go "to his sons who are living," that is, to the surviving sons; and "some of the deceased shall not inherit from others," so that the deceased son will not be deemed to have become entitled to any portion of the inheritance, and his children, as there is no right of representation in Moohummudan law, will get nothing. If, on the other hand, the less approved opinion were accepted, the children of the deceased son would be deemed to have been entitled to his portion as a residuary, and that portion would descend to his children.

THE END OF THE SIRAJIYYAH.

APPENDIX.

A. (p. 20).

"The way of knowing the agreement or disagreement between two different quantities is, that the greater be diminished by the smaller quantity on both sides, once or oftener, until they agree in one point; and if they agree in unit only, there is no numerical agreement between them; but if they agree in any number, then they are (*said to be*) *mutawafik* in a fraction, of which that number is the denominator."

Unintelligible as this may seem at first, in consequence of the extreme terseness of the phraseology and the absence of definitions of technical terms, it will be found to be a perfect and very convenient rule for finding the greatest common measure by successive subtraction, instead of finding it by division, as is usual in European arithmetic. It will thus be seen that, by two numbers agreeing in a third number (or in the fraction, i. e., reciprocal, of that number) are meant numbers having that third number for their greatest common measure.

We shall first exemplify the Arabian method by finding the agreement between twenty-eight and eight.

Twenty-eight	Eight
Twenty	Four
Twelve	
Four.	

Here, adopting, for convenience, the arrangement of a double column, and subtracting from right to left, and *vice versâ*, we have gone through the process indicated by the rule in the text. The following is an enumeration of the several steps;—Eight, subtracted from twenty-eight, leaves twenty; eight from twenty, twelve; eight from twelve, four; four from eight, four.—Now, therefore, we have the two numbers agreeing "in one point"; and, the number in which they agree being four, they are *mutawafik* in four or in one fourth.

The above remarks will enable the reader to understand the following example, which results in showing that the numbers "agree in unit only," and have therefore "no numerical agreement between them"; or, as we should express it in Europe, the numbers have no common measure but unity.

Twenty-four	Seventeen
Seven	Ten
Four	Three
One.	

The singular simplicity of this rule will probably take some European arithmeticians by surprise. It is not necessary to offer any demonstration of its correctness, except so far as to prove that it is identical in its result with the European rule for finding the g. c. m.; for our readers can find a demonstration of the last-mentioned rule in any ordinary work on algebra. In order to show clearly the identity of the results, we shall now give another example, worked out both in the Arabian and in the European manner:—

Find the agreement between fifty-five and one hundred: *and*, find the g. c. m. of 55 and 100.

Arabian method—(The reader will remember the words "once or oftener" in the Arabian rule, and will observe that several successive subtractions effect the purpose of one division):—

Fifty-five	One hundred
Ten	Forty-five
Five	Thirty-five
	Twenty-five
	Fifteen
	Five

Hence the numbers agree in five.

The process that we have gone through is as follows:—

Fifty-five subtracted from a hundred leaves forty-five; forty-five from fifty-five, ten; ten from forty-five, thirty-five; ten from thirty-five, twenty-five; ten from twenty-five, fifteen; ten from fifteen, five; five from ten, five.

European method :—

```
55) 100 (1
    55
    --
    45) 55 (1
        45
        --
        10) 45 (4
            40
            --
             5) 10 (2
                10
                ==
```

Hence, the g. c. m. of the numbers is five. It therefore appears, that when we find the agreement of two numbers by the Arabian method, the number that we arrive at as the result is the g. c. m. of the two numbers as found by the European rule.

The following is a *general* proof of the identity of result of the European and Arabian methods :—

First; find the g. c. m. of a and b by the European method.

```
a) b (x
   ax
   --
   b-ax) a          (y
         (b-ax) y
         --------
         a-(b-ax) y) b-ax           (z
                     [a-b-ax) y] z
                     =============
```

Here, it is supposed that $a-(b-ax)\ y$ is the last divisor, going exactly z times into $b-ax$, and is consequently the g. c. m. Hence :—

$$b-ax=[a-(b-ax)\ y]\ z \quad . \quad . \quad . \quad . \quad . \quad (1.)$$

Secondly; find the agreement of a and b by the Arabian method.

Remembering, from above, that a is contained in b x times with a remainder over, it is evident that in applying the Arabian method we shall subtract a from b several times, and get the successive remainders, $b-a$, $b-2a$, &c., till at last we arrive at $b-ax$, a remainder smaller than a. We shall then subtract that from a and the successive remainders in the same manner, till we arrive at the remainder $a-(b-ax)\ y$, which is smaller than $b-ax$. Lastly, we shall subtract $a-(b-ax)\ y$ from $b-ax$, and the successive remainders, till we arrive at $b-ax-[a-(b-ax)\ y]\ (z-1)$, which, if the rules are identical in their results, ought to be equal to $a-(b-ax)\ y$. The process may thus be exhibited in double columns :—

a	b
$a-(b-ax)$	$b-a$
$a-2\ (b-ax)$	$b-2a$
. . . . . .	. .
$a-(b-ax)\ y$	$b-ax$
	$b-ax-[a-(b-ax)\ y]$
	$b-ax-2\ [a-(b-ax)\ y]$
	. . . .
	$b-ax-[a-(b-ax)\ y]\ (z-1)$

We have already shown above, that in order that the results should be proved to be identical, in other words, that $a-(b-ax)\ y$, the g. c. m., may be proved to be also the agreement between the two numbers, it is necessary to show that $a-(b-ax)\ y = b-ax-[a-(b-ax)\ y]\ (z-1)$; but we have from above, (1.),

$$b-ax = [a-(b-ax)\ y]\ z$$

subtract $a-(b-ax)\ y$ from both sides, and we shall have,

$$b-ax-[a-(b-ax)\ y] = [a-(b-ax)\ y]\ (z-1)$$

or, transposing $b-ax$ and changing signs,

$$a-(b-ax)\ y = b-ax-[a\ (b-ax)\ y]\ (z-1)$$

Hence the identity of the results is clearly proved. By careful inspection, however, this proof may be rendered unnecessary, for it is plain that successive subtraction has the same practical effect as division, and therefore the two processes above exhibited may be considered almost identical; the European arithmetician recommencing his work from time to time with a fresh division, while the Arabian lawyer recommences exactly at the same stages, and with the same numbers, but subtracts instead of dividing.

B. (p. 22.)

The first principle between the shares and the persons is, "that if the portions of all the classes be divided amongst them without a fraction, there is no need of multiplication." The meaning of this will be best understood by the example given:—Father; Mother; Two Daughters—

Father, one-sixth
Mother, one-sixth
Two Daughters, two-thirds.

Here the root is six; and it is easily seen that the father takes an entire sixth, the mother an entire sixth, and each daughter two entire sixths. Consequently the sixths are delivered to the several claimants entire and unbroken; the portions, in the words of the Sirajiyyah, are "divided without a fraction," and the root need not be multiplied by any other number; in other words, the arrangement, or ultimate least common denominator, is identical with the root.

C. (p. 22.)

The second principle between the shares and the persons is, "that if the portions of one class be fractional, yet there be an agreement between their portions and their persons, then the measure of the number of persons, whose shares are broken, must be multiplied by the root of the case."*

The example given is; Father, Mother, Ten Daughters—

Father: one-sixth
Mother: one-sixth
Ten Daughters: two-thirds.

Here the root is six; but ten agrees with four,* (the daughters' portion from the root,) in two. The principle directs that the root be multiplied by the measure of ten, and the measure of ten

* Here, and elsewhere, we leave out the actual work of finding the agreement of numbers, in order to economise space.

is ten divided by two, or five.* Multiplying six by five we get thirty.

And it is clear that 30 is the l. c. d. of

$$\frac{1}{6}, \frac{1}{6}, \frac{1}{10} \text{ of } \frac{2}{3}$$
$$\text{or } \frac{1}{6}, \frac{1}{6}, \frac{1}{15}$$

D. (p. 22.)

The third principle between the shares and the persons: "If their portions leave a fraction, and there be no agreement between those portions and the persons, then the whole number of the persons whose shares are broken must be multiplied into the root of the case:" Example, wife: five sisters by the same father and mother, one paternal uncle—

Wife, one-fourth.
Five sisters, two-thirds.
Paternal uncle, residue.

The root is twelve. Five, the number of the sisters, and eight, their portion from the root, have no agreement. Consequently the root, twelve, must be multiplied by the "whole number of persons whose shares are broken," i. e., by five; and we get sixty, which is the l. c. d. of

$$\frac{1}{4}, \frac{1}{5} \text{ of } \frac{2}{3}, \frac{1}{12} \text{ (residue)}$$
$$\text{or } \frac{1}{4}, \frac{2}{15}, \frac{1}{12}$$

E. (p. 23.)

The first principle between persons and persons. "When there is a fractional division between two classes or more, but an equality between the number of the persons, then the rule is, that one

* The expression "measure of a number" is not defined; but observation and experiment shew that it is as follows:—Having found the agreement (or g. c. m.) of two numbers, divide either of those numbers by the agreement, and the quotient is the "measure" of the number so divided.

of the numbers be multiplied into the root of the case." Example; six daughters; three true grandmothers; three paternal uncles.

Six daughters, two-thirds.

Three true grandmothers, one-sixth.

Three paternal uncles, residue.

The root is six. Here at first sight it would seem that the numbers of persons were not all equal, since there are six daughters, and only three of each of the other classes. But it is tacitly assumed, though not actually stated, in the Sirajiyyah, that the six is reduced to three, as it would be if we were working out the second principle between the shares and the persons, because the daughters' portions from the root are four, and as four and six agree in two, six divided by two, or three, is the measure of six. Consequently the case is treated, for the purpose of finding the multiplier, as if the number of daughters were three, and therefore equal to the other numbers of persons. Multiplying the root by three, we get eighteen, which is the l. c. d. of:—

$$\tfrac{1}{6} \text{ of } \tfrac{2}{3},\ \tfrac{1}{3} \text{ of } \tfrac{1}{6},\ \tfrac{1}{3} \text{ of } \tfrac{1}{6} \text{ (residue)},$$

$$\text{or } \tfrac{1}{9},\ \tfrac{1}{18},\ \tfrac{1}{18}$$

F. (p. 23.)

The second principle between persons and persons: "When some of the numbers equally measure the others; then the rule is, that the greater number be multiplied into the root of the case." Example:—Four wives, three true grandmothers, twelve paternal uncles.

Four wives, one-fourth.

Three true grandmothers, one-sixth.

Twelve paternal uncles, residue.

The root is twelve. It is clear that four and three "equally measure" twelve, *i. e.*, are measures of twelve, so we must multiply the root by twelve, and we get a hundred and forty-four, which is the l. c. d. of:—

$$\tfrac{1}{4} \text{ of } \tfrac{1}{4},\ \tfrac{1}{3} \text{ of } \tfrac{1}{6},\ \tfrac{1}{12} \text{ of } \tfrac{7}{12} \text{ (residue)},$$

$$\text{or } \tfrac{1}{16},\ \tfrac{1}{18},\ \tfrac{7}{144}$$

G. (p. 23.)

The third principle between persons and persons. "When some of the numbers are *mutawafik* or composit, with others; then the rule is, that the measure of the first of the numbers be multiplied into the whole of the second, and the product into the measure of the third, if the product of the third* be *mutawafik*, or, if not, into the whole of the third, and then into the fourth, and so on, in the same manner; after which the product must be multiplied with the root of the case." Example:—Four wives, eighteen daughters, fifteen† true grandmothers, six paternal uncles.

Four wives, one-eighth.
Eighteen daughters, two-thirds.
Fifteen true grandmothers, one-sixth.
Six paternal uncles, residue.

The root is twenty-four. From what has been observed before, it will be remembered that eighteen, the number of daughters, must be reduced to nine, since eighteen agrees with sixteen (the daughters' portion from the root), in two, and nine, or eighteen divided by two, is therefore the measure of eighteen. Four and nine have no agreement, so we must (according to the spirit of the principle,) multiply four with nine, and we get thirty-six. Thirty-six and fifteen agree in three, and the measure of fifteen, or fifteen divided by three, is five. Multiplying thirty-six into five, we get one hundred and eighty. This and the fourth number, six, agree in six, so the measure of six is six divided by six, or one, and the final product is one hundred and eighty. Multiplying this into the root of the case, twenty-four, we get four thousand three hundred and twenty, which is the l. c. d. of:—

$$\tfrac{1}{4} \text{ of } \tfrac{1}{8},\ \tfrac{1}{18} \text{ of } \tfrac{2}{3},\ \tfrac{1}{15} \text{ of } \tfrac{1}{6},\ \tfrac{1}{6} \text{ of } \tfrac{1}{24} \text{ (residue)},$$

$$\text{or, } \tfrac{1}{32},\ \tfrac{1}{27},\ \tfrac{1}{90},\ \tfrac{1}{144}$$

* This should be "the product *and* the third," for the word "of" is unmeaning here, and the working out of the principle enables us to see clearly that it is the agreement between the product and the next number that we have to ascertain.

† This is an impossible case, for we should have to ascend fifteen generations to get fifteen true female ancestors on a level (so to speak); who would inherit together. It is given, however, as an example, in the Sirajiyyah.

H. (p. 23.)

The fourth principle between persons and persons : " When the numbers are *mutabáyan*, or not agreeing with one another ; and then the rule is, that the first of the numbers be multiplied into the whole of the second, and the product multiplied by the whole of the third, and that product into the whole of the fourth, and the last product into the root of the case." Example ; two wives, six true grandmothers, ten daughters, and seven paternal uncles.

Two wives, one-eighth.
Six true grandmothers, one-sixth.
Ten daughters, two-thirds.
Seven paternal uncles, residue.

Here again the root is twenty-four. As before, the number of the daughters must be divided by two, and becomes five. Two and six agree in two, and the measure of six is three. These have no agreement with five or seven, and five and seven have no agreement with one another, so we must multiply two, three, five, and seven together, and we get two hundred and ten. Multiplying this product into the root, we get five thousand and forty,* which is the l. c. d. of :—

$$\tfrac{1}{2} \text{ of } \tfrac{1}{8}, \ \tfrac{1}{6} \text{ of } \tfrac{1}{6}, \ \tfrac{1}{10} \text{ of } \tfrac{2}{3}, \ \tfrac{1}{7} \text{ of } \tfrac{1}{24} \text{ (residue)};$$
$$\text{or, } \tfrac{1}{16}, \ \tfrac{1}{36}, \ \tfrac{1}{15}, \ \tfrac{1}{168}$$

I. (p. 24.)

In applying the above "principles" we must always be careful to consider the portions from the root of the case, and to begin by ascertaining whether the second principle between shares and persons is applicable. It is rather singular that the examples in the Sirajiyyah only shew the applicability of this principle to the

* It will be perceived that this example belongs, partially, to the previous principle. A better example, strictly speaking, of this last principle, would be : three wives, four true grandmothers, five daughters, and seven paternal uncles ; where none of the numbers have any agreement with one another.

share two-thirds, but it is evident that it is required for other shares also. Thus, if we have:—

One wife, one-eighth.
Two daughters, two-thirds.
Ten true grandmothers, one-sixth.
One paternal uncle, residue.

The root is twenty-four. The grandmothers' portion from the root is four, and four and ten agree in two, therefore the measure of the number of true grandmothers is five. If we forget this we shall multiply the root by ten, and get two hundred and forty; whereas it is clear, that 120, or 24 × 5, is the l. c. d. of:—

$$\tfrac{1}{8},\ \tfrac{1}{2} \text{ of } \tfrac{2}{3},\ \tfrac{1}{10} \text{ of } \tfrac{1}{6},\ \tfrac{1}{24} \text{ (residue)};$$

$$\text{or, } \tfrac{1}{8},\ \tfrac{1}{3},\ \tfrac{1}{60},\ \tfrac{1}{24}$$

J. (p. 24.)

"When thou desirest to know the share of each class by arrangement, multiply what each class has from the root of the case by what thou hast already multiplied into the root of the case, and the product is the share of that class."

To show the working of this rule, we shall take the case given in the Sirajiyyah to illustrate the third principle between persons and persons; viz.—Four wives, eighteen daughters, fifteen true grandmothers, and six paternal uncles. It will be remembered that the root is twenty-four; and it is easily ascertained by inspection that the portions of the classes from the root of the case* are:—

Wives, three.
Daughters, sixteen.
True grandmothers, four.
Paternal uncles, one.

* By the expression "what each class has from the root of the case" is meant, as will be clearly seen by those who work out the following example, the numerator of the fraction accruing to each class (as wives, daughters, &c.), so long as the divisor or root is treated as the l. c. d.

Multiplying by one hundred and eighty, the number which we have previously multiplied into the root of the case, we get :—

Wives, five hundred and forty.

Daughters, two thousand eight hundred and eighty.

True grandmothers, seven hundred and twenty.

Paternal uncles, one hundred and eighty.

According to European arithmetic, the shares of the classes being (from above),—

Wives, $\frac{1}{8}$

Daughters, $\frac{2}{3}$

True grandmothers, $\frac{1}{6}$

Paternal uncles, $\frac{1}{24}$

It will necessarily follow that if we divide the whole into 4320 parts, we shall get for the several classes* :—

Wives, $\frac{1}{8}$ of $4320 = 540$.

Daughters, $\frac{2}{3}$ of $4320 = 2880$.

True grandmothers, $\frac{1}{6}$ of $4320 = 720$.

Paternal uncles, $\frac{1}{24}$ of $4320 = 180$.

K. (p. 24.)

"If thou desirest to know the share of each individual in that class by arrangement, divide what each class has from the principle of the case by the number of persons in it†. . . . . Another method is, to divide the multiplied number by whichever class thou thinkest proper, then to multiply the quotient into the

* It is perhaps almost unnecessary to remark that in Europe we should not think it necessary to exhibit the shares of the classes, but should at once go on to find the shares of individuals, viz. :—$\frac{1}{32}$, $\frac{1}{27}$, $\frac{1}{90}$, and $\frac{1}{144}$ of 4320.

† Here follow the words :—"Then multiply the quotient into the multiplicand." There must be some error here in the translation or in the text from which it is taken ; for it is clear, whatever these words may signify, that they are unnecessary, as we shall already have ascertained the share of the individual by dividing what the class has from the principle of the case by the number of individuals in the class.

share of that set, by which thou hast divided the multiplied number. . . . . Another method is by the way of proportion, which is the clearest; and it is, that a proportion be ascertained for the share of each class from the root of the case to the number of persons one by one, and that, according to such proportion, from the multiplied number, a share be given to each individual of that class."

To illustrate these three methods we shall continue working out the example which was brought up to a certain point in Appendix J.

First method :—

Four wives taking five hundred and forty parts from the principle of the case, each wife takes five hundred and forty divided by four, or one hundred and thirty-five. Similarly, each of the eighteen daughters takes two thousand eight hundred and eighty divided by eighteen, or one hundred and sixty; each of the fifteen true grandmothers, seven hundred and twenty divided by fifteen, or forty-eight; each of the six paternal uncles, one hundred and eighty divided by six, or thirty.

Second method :—

The "multiplied number" is the number "multiplied into the root of the case," i. e., one hundred and eighty.

For each wife, divide by four, the number of wives, and multiply by three, the share* from the root of the case; and we get one hundred and thirty-five.

For each daughter, divide by eighteen, and multiply by sixteen, and we get one hundred and sixty.

For each true grandmother, divide by fifteen, and multiply by four, and we get forty-eight.

For each paternal uncle, divide by six, and multiply by one, and we get thirty.

Third method :—

The share of the wives from the root of the case is three; the number of wives, four. The proportion, or rather the ratio, is three to four. We have now to find the number which has the

* The Sirajiyyah merely says, "the share of that set," but it is evident that the "share from the root of the case" is meant; for if we multiplied by the share "from the principle of the case" we should make the ultimate share of each individual larger than that of the entire class to which he belongs.

same ratio to one hundred and eighty that three has to four, and it is easily ascertained that this is one hundred and thirty-five.

The portion of the individuals of the other classes will be found in the same way.*

L. (p. 26.)

"Now, as to the payment of debts, the debts of all the creditors stand in the place of the arranging number." It will be remembered that debts are paid before the distribution of the estate among the relations can take place (see p. 2). Consequently, when the estate is sufficient to pay all the creditors, they take, in full, the sums due to them, and there is no necessity for any rule of distribution among them. The rule above stated is therefore required only when the estate is insufficient for entire payment of the debts, in which case it furnishes, in connection with what has been learnt from the previous portion of the work, a perfect guide for dividing the property among the creditors in the exact proportion of the amounts actually due to them respectively. This will be best explained by an example:—

A man dies, leaving an estate of four hundred gold mohurs.

* The "third method" clearly points to some mechanical mode of ascertaining a fourth proportional. In Europe we are so accustomed to do this by multiplying and dividing, that we are apt to forget that proportion is an intrinsic mechanical relation of things, and that the arithmetical processes of multiplication and division are only the means of ascertaining it. The mechanical mode used by the Arabians may perhaps have been as follows:—

Let A B, A C, be two graduated rods inclined to one another at any angle, and joined at A. From D, the third degree of A B, stretch a string to E, the fourth degree of A C. Now from F, the hundred and eightieth degree of A C, stretch a string parallel to E D, meeting A B in G. A G will be to A F as A D to A E (as we know from the principles of geometry), and it will be found that G is the hundred and thirty-fifth degree of A B, so that the fourth proportional, one hundred and thirty-five, will be ascertained.

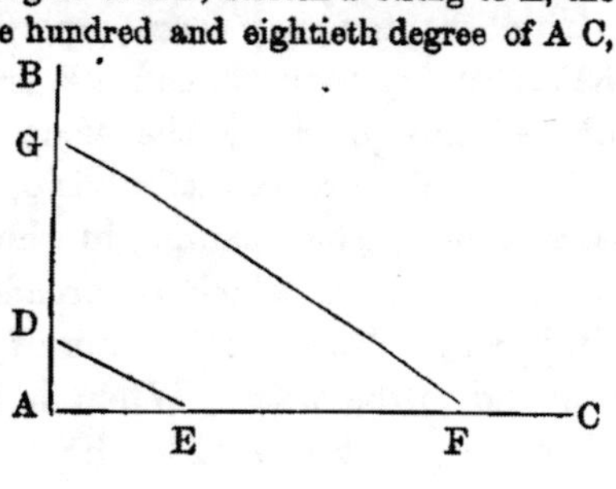

There are three creditors, one of whom claims three hundred, another, two hundred, a third, one hundred. It is evident that the estate is insufficient to pay all three claims, and all the debts, in English legal phraseology, must "abate," so that each creditor may receive his due proportion, We have, then :—

First creditor, three hundred.
Second creditor, two hundred.
Third creditor, one hundred.

In order to find the arrangement we add these sums together, and we get six hundred. This will be the denominator of all the fractions. The numerators are the several numbers, three hundred, two hundred, and one hundred; and the estate will be divided among the creditors as follows :—

First creditor; three hundred six hundredths.
Second creditor ; two hundred six hundredths.
Third creditor ; one hundred six hundredths.

This rule, almost unexampled, even in the Sirajiyyah, in brevity of expression, is identical with the rule of "proportionate parts," which may be found stated and exemplified in any European treatise on Algebra or Arithmetic. The property is exactly divided, since the sum of the numerators is exactly equal to the denominator; and it is divided in due proportions, because there is a common denominator, and therefore the fractions are to each other in the ratio of the numerators, that is, in the ratio of the debts of the several creditors.

M. (p. 27.)

This chapter may seem superfluous, as it only amounts to this, that if one person takes his share before the general division, the others take precisely the same portions that they would have if the whole process of division were effected, as usual, at the same time. The example in the text involves an allusion to the law of dower, of which the reader will find no explanation in the Sirajiyyah. Dower is a sum of money given *or promised* by the husband to the wife. When it is not actually given at the time of marriage, it is said to be "deferred," and the problem here proposed is an example of the division of deferred dower. Dower is the absolute property of the wife, and descends like any other property that she may possess. In the case proposed, we have accordingly:—

Husband, one-half.
Mother, one-third.
Paternal uncle, residue.

It is clear, therefore, that if the husband retains his moiety (or, as stated in the text, "agrees to take what was in his power"), one-half remains; and as one-half is equal to three-sixths, the mother will take two-sixths (or one-third), and the uncle one-sixth; "and thus," in the words of the text, "there will be two parts for the mother" (*i. e.*, of what remains after the husband's share is subtracted), "and one for the uncle." The case is so simple that we have not thought it necessary to work it out with the usual formalities of finding the divisor, &c.; and our only reason for offering any explanation of this and some other passages of slight importance is, that the rules given in the text, by their extreme terseness and apparent want of connection with other parts of the work, might, if passed over without explanation, lead the reader to suppose that some new process was indicated.

N. (p. 27.)

The calculation of the return is sometimes complicated by the presence of a husband or wife, who is not allowed to partake of it. The point that we have to arrive at is, of course, the division of the whole property, (or, as the case may be, the whole remaining property after payment of the husband or wife), among the sharers in proportion to the amount of their shares from the root. The Sirajiyyah classifies cases of return in four divisions:—

First division: "When there is in the case but one sort of kinsmen to whom a return must be made, and none of those who are not entitled to a return; then settle the case according to the number of persons." Example. Two daughters. Settle by two; *i. e.*, substitute two for three, which would otherwise be the root of the case.

Second division: "When there are joined in the case two or three sorts of those, to whom a return must be made, without any of those, to whom there is no return: then settle the case, ... by two if there be two sixths in the case; or by three, when there are a third and a sixth in it, or by four, when there are a moiety and a sixth in it; or by five, when there are in it two thirds and a sixth, or a half and two sixths, or a half and a third."

It is easy to see that in these two divisions we simply use the converse process of the increase; that is to say, that we diminish the divisor, (instead of increasing it), so as to make it equal to the aggregate number of parts from the root. Thus if we have:—

Two thirds,
One sixth,

The root is six; but the shares from the root are four and one, which together make five; consequently the root is reduced to five. It is clear that here, as in the increase, the relative value of the shares remains undisturbed.

Third division: When there is only one class entitled to the return, and there is also a person (husband or wife) who takes no return. "Then give the share of him or her, to whom there is no return, according to the lowest denominator,* and if the residue exactly quadrate with the number of persons who are entitled to a return, it is well; . . . . but if they do not agree, then multiply the measure of the number of the persons, if there be an agreement between the number of persons and the residue, into the denominator of the shares of those, to whom no return is to be made; if not, multiply the whole number of persons into the denominator of the share of those, to whom there is no return; and the product will set the case right."

Here are three cases, which, notwithstanding some confusion and obscurity of language, can be made out without much difficulty. Example (first case), husband; three daughters.

Husband, one fourth.

Three daughters, two thirds.

* This word is not in the text of the original, and perhaps "denomination" would be a better word to introduce. It means, in fact, not the root of the case, but the denominator of the primary share of the husband or wife.

The case of the persons who take a return is to be settled according to the number of persons; *i. e.*, the case is three. Now we give the husband " his share according to the lowest denominator," *i. e.*, we suppose a division into four parts and we give him one, and there are three parts remaining. But this residue exactly quadrates with (*i. e.*, is equal to) the number of daughters; so, " it is well," *i. e.*, we retain four as the root, without multiplying.

Example (second case); husband, six daughters.

Husband, one-fourth.

Six daughters, two-thirds.

The case is six. Proceeding as before, we find that the residue after paying the husband is three, which agrees with six, the number of daughters, in three. Therefore the measure of six is six divided by three, or two, so we must multiply four by two, and we get eight.

Example, (third case); husband, ten daughters.

Husband, one-fourth.

Ten daughters, two-thirds.

The case is ten; and three is not equal to ten, and has no agreement with ten. Consequently we must multiply four by ten, and we get forty.

In the cases of return above given, the shares will be found in the usual way; the denominator last found being treated as the arrangement, and the primary share of the person who takes no return being treated as the root. Thus in the third case we have:—

Husband (from the root), one.

Ten daughters (from the root), three.

Multiplying by ten, and afterwards, in the case of the daughters, dividing by ten to obtain the shares of individuals, we have:—

Husband, ten.

Ten daughters, thirty; each, three.

Fourth division:—When there are several classes entitled to the return, and there is also a person (husband or wife) who takes no return. " Then divide what remains from the denominator of the share of him or them,* who have no return, by the case of

* There may, of course, be several wives, though there can only be one husband.

those, to whom a return must be made, and if the remainder quadrate, it is well; and this is one form . . . . but, if it do not quadrate, then multiply the whole case of those, who are entitled to a return, into the denominator of the share of him or her who is not entitled to it; and the product will be the denominator of the shares of both classes."

Here we have two cases. Example, (first case), wife, true grandmother, two half-sisters by the mother's side.

Wife, one fourth.
True grandmother, one sixth.
Two half-sisters, one third.

The case of those who partake in the return is three, and we have to divide by it "what remains from the denominator &c.," *i. e.*, three; and we find that it exactly quadrates. Consequently "it is well;" the number four, without any multiplication, is to be treated as the root.

Example, (second case), four wives, nine daughters, six true grandmothers.

Four wives, one eighth.
Nine daughters, two thirds.
Six true grandmothers, one sixth.

The case of those who are entitled to a return is five, and this does not quadrate with seven, the quantity which "remains from the denominator" of the wives' share. Therefore we must multiply the denominator eight by five, and we get forty; which must be treated as the root.

To find out the ultimate shares of classes and individuals in cases of return included in the "third division" and "fourth division," we must apply the usual principles of arrangement, treating as the root the number already obtained by multiplying the denominator of the person who takes no return.* Thus, from the last example, as four and nine have no agreement, we multiply four by nine, and we get thirty-six. This is exactly measured by six, so we must multiply the root by thirty-six, and we get, for the whole number of parts, one thousand four hundred and forty.

* This, it will readily be perceived, is the meaning of the injunction in the text; "if there be a fraction in some, adjust the case by the before mentioned principles," (see p. 29).

The shares of classes from the root are:—

Four wives, five.

Nine daughters, twenty-eight.

Six true grandmothers, seven.

Multiplying by thirty-six for the classes, and then dividing by the respective numbers of the individuals, we get:—

Four wives; one hundred and eighty; each, forty-five.

Nine daughters; one thousand and eight; each, one hundred and twelve.

Six true grandmothers; two hundred and fifty-two; each, forty-two.

By European arithmetic the same results will be obtained. Thus, taking the last example, we have:—

4 wives; $\frac{1}{8}$; each, $\frac{1}{32}$

9 daughters and 6 true grandmothers; $\frac{7}{8}$, to be divided in the ratio $\frac{2}{3} : \frac{1}{6}$, or $4 : 1$; hence;

9 daughters; $\frac{4}{5}$ of $\frac{7}{8} = \frac{7}{10}$; each, $\frac{1}{9}$ of $\frac{7}{10} = \frac{7}{90}$

6 true grandmothers; $\frac{1}{5}$ of $\frac{7}{8} = \frac{7}{40}$; each, $\frac{1}{6}$ of $\frac{7}{40} = \frac{7}{240}$

Reducing, $\frac{1}{32}$, $\frac{7}{90}$, $\frac{7}{240}$ to the l. c. d., we have,

Each wife; $\frac{45}{1440}$

Each daughter; $\frac{112}{1440}$

Each true grandmother; $\frac{42}{1440}$

O. (p. 33.)

The rule for calculating vested inheritances is as follows: "That the case of the first deceased be arranged, and that the allotment of each heir be considered as delivered according to that arrangement; that, next, the case of the second deceased be arranged, and that a comparison be made between what was in his hands, or vested in interest, from the first arrangement, in three situations; * and if, on account of equality, what is in his hands from

* The words "in three situations" merely signify that one of three cases will occur, according to circumstances, namely, equality, agreement, or disagreement.

the first arrangement graduate with the second arrangement, then there is no need of multiplication; but, if it be not right, then see whether there is an agreement between the two, and multiply the measure of the second arrangement into the whole of the first arrangement; and, if there be a disagreement between them, then multiply the whole of the second arrangement into the whole of the first arrangement, and the product will be the denominator of both cases. The allotments of the heirs of the first deceased must be multiplied into the former multiplicand, I mean into the second arrangement or into its measure; and the allotments of the heirs of the second deceased must be multiplied into the whole of what was in his hands, or into its measure; and if a third or fourth die, put the second product in the place of the first arrangement, and the third case in the place of the second, in working; and thus in the case of a fourth and a fifth, and so on to infinities." Example; A woman (the "first deceased," *i.e.*, the *proposita*) leaves husband, daughter, mother; husband dies before distribution, leaving wife, father, and mother; their daughter dies, leaving two sons, daughter, and maternal grandmother; lastly grandmother dies, leaving husband and two brothers.

From the first deceased we have :—

Husband, one-fourth.
Daughter, one-half.
Mother, one-sixth.

The root is twelve, and this is a case of return, since the shares from the root, three, six, and two, only amount to eleven.

The case of those who are entitled to the return is four; the residue from the share of the husband, who does not partake of the return, is three, which does not quadrate with four, so we must multiply four, the denominator of the person who has no return, by four, the case of those who take the return, and we get sixteen.

Sixteen is therefore the first arrangement, and the allotments out of it are :—

Husband, four.
Daughter, nine.
Mother, three.

The husband is the second deceased, and he leaves, daughter (who is his own daughter as well as that of the *proposita*), wife, mother, father. We have now to find, first of all, the second arrangement and the allotments from it, *i. e.* the shares of the estate of the second deceased among his heirs without reference to the first deceased and her estate.

We have:—

Daughter; one-half.
H.'s wife; one-eighth.
H.'s mother; one-sixth.
H.'s father; residue.

The root is twenty-four, and twenty-four is also the second arrangement, since none of the shares are broken, so that the principles of arrangement do not require us to multiply the root. Now four, the allotment in the husband's hands from the first arrangement, does not quadrate with twenty-four, but they agree in four, so the measure of the second arrangement is twenty-four divided by four, or six. Multiplying the first arrangement, sixteen, by six, we get ninety-six. Multiplying the allotments of the heirs of the first deceased by six, and leaving those of the heirs of the second deceased (*i. e.* their shares from the root twenty-four) untouched, since the measure of four is four divided by four, or one, we get:—

Daughter; sixty-six.
Mother; eighteen.
H.'s wife; three.
H.'s mother; four.
H.'s father; five (residue).

It will be observed that the daughter's allotment from the first deceased, nine, became fifty-four when multiplied by six; and her allotment from the second deceased, twelve, when added to fifty-four, makes up the above-mentioned number, sixty-six. Of the other heirs, the mother of the first deceased, not being related to the second deceased, takes nothing from him; the rest, not being related to the first deceased, take nothing but the allotments from the second deceased. It is therefore only in the case of the daughter that two allotments have to be added together.

Next, the daughter dies, leaving, two sons, a daughter, maternal grandmother; and it must be remembered also that H.'s mother and H.'s father are her paternal grandmother and paternal grandfather.

H's mother; one-sixth.

H's father; one-sixth.

D's maternal grandmother; one-sixth.

D's two sons and one daughter, (equal to five daughters); residue.

The root is six, and the principles of arrangement require multiplication by five, so we get thirty as the third arrangement. Sixty-six, the quantity in the daughter's hands from the second arrangement, does not quadrate with thirty, but they agree in six, and therefore the measure of thirty is five. Multiplying the product from the second arrangement, ninety-six, by five, we get four hundred and eighty as the product from the third arrangement. Multiplying the allotments previously obtained by five, the measure of thirty, and those from the third arrangement by eleven, the measure of sixty-six, and adding where necessary, we get:—

Mother; ninety.
H's wife; fifteen.
H's mother; seventy-five.
H's father; eighty.
D's maternal grandmother; fifty-five.
D's sons (each); sixty-six.
D's daughter; thirty-three.

Lastly, the daughter's maternal grandmother dies, leaving a *second* husband* and two brothers:—

D's mat. grandmother's husband; one-half.
D's mat. grandmother's two brothers; residue.

The root is two; and by the principles of arrangement this must be multiplied by two, the number of brothers, and we get four as the fourth arrangement. Fifty-five, the quantity in the daughter's maternal grandmother's hands from the third arrangement, does not quadrate with four, and has no agreement with it, so we must multiply four into the product from the third arrangement, four hundred and eighty, and we get one thousand nine hundred and twenty. Multiply the allotments previously obtained by four, and those from the last arrangement by fifty-five, we get:—

* *i. e.*, not the daughter's maternal grandfather, for otherwise he would have been mentioned as one of the daughter's heirs.

Mother; three hundred and sixty.

H's wife; sixty.

H's mother; three hundred.

H's father; three hundred and twenty.

D's sons, (each); two hundred and sixty-four.

D's daughter; one hundred and thirty-two.

D's mat. grandmother's husband; one hundred and ten.

D's mat. grandmother's brothers, (each); fifty-five.

In this last stage there is no necessity for addition, since the heirs of the last deceased are not heirs of any previously deceased person.

This case may be thus worked out by European arithmetic :—

Husband; $\frac{1}{4}$

Daughter and mother, $\frac{3}{4}$, to be divided in the ratio $\frac{1}{2} : \frac{1}{6}$ or $3 : 1$

$\therefore$ Daughter, $\frac{3}{4}$ of $\frac{3}{4} = \frac{9}{16}$

Mother, $\frac{1}{4}$ of $\frac{3}{4} = \frac{3}{16}$

Husband dies, leaving the daughter; a wife; a mother, and a father.

Daughter; $\frac{9}{16} + \frac{1}{2}$ of $\frac{1}{4} = \frac{9}{16} + \frac{1}{8} = \frac{11}{16}$

Mother; $\frac{3}{16}$

H's wife; $\frac{1}{8}$ of $\frac{1}{4} = \frac{1}{32}$

H's mother; $\frac{1}{6}$ of $\frac{1}{4} = \frac{1}{24}$

H's father; $\frac{1}{4} - \frac{19}{96} = \frac{5}{96}$*

Daughter dies, leaving H's father, her paternal grandfather; H's mother, her paternal grandmother; maternal grandmother; two sons; daughter.

Mother; $\frac{3}{16}$

H's wife; $\frac{1}{32}$

H's mother; $\frac{1}{24} + \frac{1}{6}$ of $\frac{11}{16} = \frac{1}{24} + \frac{11}{96} = \frac{15}{96}$

H's father; $\frac{5}{96} + \frac{1}{6}$ of $\frac{11}{16} = \frac{5}{96} + \frac{11}{96} = \frac{1}{6}$

D's mat. grandmother; $\frac{1}{6}$ of $\frac{11}{16} = \frac{11}{96}$

D's two sons (each); $\frac{2}{5}$ of $\frac{11}{32}$† $= \frac{11}{80}$

D's daughter; $\frac{1}{5}$ of $\frac{11}{32} = \frac{11}{160}$

* This is the residue of the husband's share after deducting the portions taken by his other heirs.

† This is the residue of the daughter's share after deducting the portions taken by her three grandparents.

Lastly, D's maternal grandmother dies, leaving a second husband and two brothers.

Mother; $\frac{3}{16}$
H's wife; $\frac{1}{32}$
H's mother; $\frac{15}{96}$
H's father; $\frac{1}{6}$
D's two sons (each); $\frac{11}{80}$
D's daughter; $\frac{11}{160}$
D's mat. grandmother's husband; $\frac{1}{2}$ of $\frac{11}{96} = \frac{11}{192}$
D's mat. grandmother's two brothers, (each); $\frac{1}{2}$ of $\frac{11}{192}$* $= \frac{11}{384}$

Reducing these fractions to the l. c. d. we get .—

Mother, $\frac{360}{1920}$
H's wife, $\frac{60}{1920}$
H's mother, $\frac{300}{1920}$
H's father, $\frac{320}{1920}$
D's two sons (each), $\frac{264}{1920}$
D's daughter, $\frac{132}{1920}$
D's mat. grandmother's husband, $\frac{110}{1920}$
D's mat. grandmother's two brothers (each), $\frac{55}{1920}$

We shall now give another case of vested inheritance, the most complicated that we have as yet met with. This particular case is important, as showing the want of power of the Arabian methods, not, indeed, to produce an accurate result, but to exhibit the result in all cases with the least common denominator.

Wife; *by her*, three sons, B, C, D; and two daughters, E, F; *by another wife*, a daughter, G. The wife, B, C, and G die successively before distribution.

Wife, one eighth.
Three sons, and three daughters (equal to nine daughters), residue.

The root is eight. Now seven, the portion of the sons and daughters from the root, has no agreement with nine, therefore

* This is the residue of the daughter's maternal grandmother's share after deducting the share taken by her husband.

nine must be multiplied into the root, and we get for the first arrangement, seventy-two. The allotments from the first arrangement are :—

Wife ; one multiplied by nine, or nine.

Three sons, and three daughters ; seven multiplied by nine, or sixty-three.

Each daughter ; sixty-three divided by nine, or seven.

Each son ; twice seven, or fourteen.

Wife dies, leaving three sons, and two daughters. G, who is not *her* daughter, takes nothing from her.

Three sons and two daughters (equal to eight daughters) ; residue.

The root is one, since there are no sharers ; eight and one have no agreement, so one must be multiplied by eight, and we get eight as the second arrangement. The original portions from the second arrangement are :—

Three sons and two daughters, eight.

Each daughter, eight divided by eight, or one.

Each son, twice one, or two.

Now nine was the quantity in the wife's hands from the first arrangement, and between this and the second arrangement there is no agreement ; so the whole of the second arrangement, eight, must be multiplied into the whole of the first arrangement, seventy-two ; and we get five hundred and seventy-six.

The allotments of the heirs of the first deceased must be multiplied by eight, and we get :—

B, C, D (each) ; one hundred and twelve.

E, F (each) ; fifty-six.

G ; fifty-six.

The allotments of the heirs from the second arrangement must be multiplied by what was in the wife's hands, nine, and we get :—

B, C, D (each) ; eighteen.

E, F (each) ; nine.

Adding, where necessary, we get :—

B, C, D (each) ; one hundred and thirty.

E, F (each) ; sixty-five.

G ; fifty-six.

Now B dies, leaving two brothers, C, D; two sisters, E, F; his half-sister, G, is excluded.

Two brothers, and two sisters (equal to six sisters); residue.

The root is one, since there are no sharers. Six and one have no agreement, so we multiply one by six, and we get six as the third arrangement. The original portions from the third arrangement are:—

Two brothers and two sisters, six.

Each sister, six divided by six, or one.

Each brother, twice one, or two.

Now one hundred and thirty was the quantity in B's hands from the second arrangement, and this agrees with the third arrangement, six, in two, so the measure of the third arrangement, three, must be multiplied into the whole of the second arrangement, by which we must now understand, the product or ultimate form of the second arrangement, five hundred and seventy-six; and we get one thousand seven hundred and twenty-eight.

The allotments of the heirs from the second arrangement must be multiplied by the measure of the third arrrangement, three, and we get:—

C, D (each); three hundred and ninety.

E, F (each); one hundred and ninety-five.

G; one hundred and sixty-eight.

The allotments of the heirs from the third arrangement must be multiplied by the measure of what was in B's hands from the second arrangement, *i. e.*, by one hundred and thirty divided by two, or sixty-five, and we get,

C, D, (each); one hundred and thirty.

E, F, (each); sixty-five.

Adding where necessary, we get,

C, D, (each); five hundred and twenty.

E, F, (each); two hundred and sixty.

G; one hundred and sixty-eight.

Next, C dies, leaving one brother, D; two sisters, E, F; G is again excluded.

Brother and two sisters (equal to four sisters); residue.

The root, as before, is one, and it must be multiplied by four, so we get four for the fourth arrangement. The original shares from the fourth arrangement are :—

Brother and two sisters, four.

Each sister, four divided by four, or one.

Brother, twice one, or two.

Five hundred and twenty, the quantity in C's hands from the third arrangement, agrees with four in four; so the measure of five hundred and twenty is one hundred and thirty, and the measure of four is one. Proceeding as before, we get for the product simply the same number as the product of the third arrangement (since we only have to multiply by one), one thousand seven hundred and twenty-eight.

Allotments of heirs from the third arrangement, multiplied by one, remain as before :—

D ; five hundred and twenty.

E, F, (each) ; two hundred and sixty.

G ; one hundred and sixty-eight.

Allotments of heirs from fourth arrangement, multiplied by the measure of five hundred and twenty, or one hundred and thirty ;

D ; Two hundred and sixty.

E, F, (each) ; one hundred and thirty.

Adding where necessary :—

D ; seven hundred and eighty.

E, F, (each) ; three hundred and ninety.

G ; one hundred and sixty-eight.

Lastly, G dies, leaving one half-brother, D, and two sisters, E, F, who succeed to her property in default of brothers and sisters of the whole blood.

Brother and two sisters (equal to four sisters), residue.

Root, one ; fifth arrangement, one multiplied by four, or four.

Original shares from the fifth arrangement :—

Each sister ; one.

Brother ; two.

One hundred and sixty-eight, the quantity in G's hands from the fourth arrangement, agrees with four in four ; so the respective measures are forty-two and one. The product will still be one thousand seven hundred and twenty-eight.

Allotments of heirs from the fourth arrangement remain as before : —

D; seven hundred and eighty.

E, F, (each); three hundred and ninety.

Allotments of heirs from the fifth arrangement, multiplied by forty-two;

D; eighty-four.

E, F, (each); forty-two.

Adding where necessary, we get, as the ultimate portions of the survivors:—

D; eight hundred and sixty-four.

E, F; (each); four hundred and thirty-two.

This last problem is worked out by European arithmetic in Rums. Ch., p. 35; and it there appears that the ultimate portions are $\frac{2}{4}$, $\frac{1}{4}$; which are, in fact, identical with $\frac{864}{1728}$, $\frac{432}{1728}$. In this instance, therefore, the Arabian method does not give us the *least* common denominator. This may often happen in cases of vested inheritance, for the addition of the portions derived from the persons who successively die may produce unforeseen combinations of numbers. The European arithmetician, at every stage of calculation, reduces his fractions to their lowest terms; but for this the old Arabian arithmeticians appear to have had no provision. Consequently, if the earlier arrangements gave them a large denominator, they had no means of diminishing it, but were compelled to remain encumbered with it to the end. Cases of vested inheritance, however, are the only problems of Mahommedan inheritance in which the methods of the Sirajiyyah, if properly applied, can fail to exhibit the ultimate portions with the least common denominator.

P. (pp. 35, 36.)

Supposing that the only relations left are a daughter's son and a daughter's daughter. Here the male will take two-thirds, and the female one-third, according to the general rule which gives a double portion to the male. But if, on the other hand, there be only a daughter of a daughter's son, and a son of a daughter's daughter, thus:—

Propositus.

Daughter. — Daughter

Daughter's son — Daughter's daughter

Daughter's son's daughter — Daughter's daughter's son.

Then a contest arises as to the portions that the surviving great-grandchildren are to take; one party maintaining that the male is to take two-thirds, on account of his sex, the other, (with whom the author of the Sirajiyyah seems to agree), that the sex of the grandson, as compared with that of the granddaughter, ought to decide the question, so that the female, on account of her father's sex, will take two-thirds, and the male, on account of the inferior sex of the parent through whom he traces his relationship, will only take one-third

---

Q. (p. 51.)

This rule, with the aid of the example given, will be easily understood by those who have mastered the previous portions of the work, and have become acquainted with its peculiar arithmetical phraseology. The example is thus worked out:—

Father, one sixth.
Mother, one sixth.
Daughter, one half.
Wife, one eighth.
Sons (unborn), residuaries.

or,

Daughters (unborn), taking two-thirds with the other daughter.

Suppose, first, that the unborn children will be sons; then the divisor is twenty-four. Suppose, secondly, that the unborn child will be a daughter; then we shall have, primarily, twenty-four for the divisor; but the shares will be four, four, sixteen, (the share of two daughters being two-thirds), and three, or twenty-seven. Consequently it is a case of increase, and the divisor will be twenty-seven.

Twenty-four and twenty-seven agree in three, therefore, according to the rule given in the text, we must multiply the measure of one of the divisors into the whole of the other (*i. e.* eight into twenty-seven, or nine into twenty-four), and we get two hundred and sixteen. This number is the arrangement of the case, and we get, multiplying the portions from the root (except the daughter's), first by nine, and then by eight :—

Father ; thirty-six.
Mother ; thirty-six.
Wife ; twenty-seven.

And :—

Father ; thirty-two.
Mother ; thirty-two.
Wife ; twenty-four.

The smaller shares thus ascertained are given at once, and the excess of the larger over the smaller is reserved, that is to say, four parts from each parent's share, and three parts from the wife's.

The above application of the rules already known is simple enough, but with regard to the daughter's share the working of the rule is more complicated.

On the supposition that there will be sons, there will be only one daughter. It is supposed by the Arabian Jurists that there may be four sons at a birth ; and therefore enough must be kept back to meet their possible claims. The daughter will be made a residuary by the sons, and she can only take, in such case, one half of what each son takes, or one ninth of the whole residue. Consequently, as we have at present disposed of eighty-eight two hundred and sixteenths, and have reserved eleven, so that there are only one hundred and seventeen to be considered, we have :—

Daughter ; one-ninth of one hundred and seventeen, or thirteen.

We have therefore reserved ;

Out of the father's share ; four.
„ mother's „ four.
„ wife's „ three.
„ daughter's „ one hundred and seventeen, less thirteen, or one hundred and four.

Or one hundred and fifteen in all.

The concluding paragraph of the chapter shows how the reserved portions are to be disposed of, according to the various eventualities that may occur. If the wife bring forth a daughter or daughters, then she or they, with the elder daughter, being entitled (as seen above) to sixteen from the root, will take from the arrangement, sixteen multiplied by eight, or one hundred and twenty-eight, which will make, in all, one hundred and twenty-eight two hundred and sixteenths, or sixteen twenty-sevenths. The other heirs, in this case, will not recover any of the reserved portions, since the whole is exhausted. We know, from the early part of the case, that this should be so, and we find that it is so, since thirteen, the portion given to the elder daughter, and one hundred and fifteen, the entire portion reserved, together make up exactly one hundred and twenty-eight.

On the other hand, if there are sons, they will be residuaries, and the father, mother, and wife will take their shares in full, that is to say, they will recover the reserved portions, before the residue is divided; and, of course, the daughter will be a residuary, and will take half as much as each son. If there are four sons, the thirteen already paid will be her just share, but if not, she must receive so much more as the circumstances render necessary. Lastly, if the child be born dead, the father, mother, and wife will recover the portions reserved from their shares, the daughter, being, on this supposition, entitled to twelve from the root twenty-four, will take twelve multiplied by nine, or one hundred and eight, from the arrangement. This (inclusive, of course, of her thirteen already received), will obviously be her proper share, one half. The father, it will be remembered, is a residuary as well as a sharer, since there are no sons. He will, therefore, in addition to the thirty-six parts already received, take the nine parts that are left, after payment of thirty-six, thirty-six, twenty-seven, and a hundred and eight, the shares above calculated. Consequently he will receive thirty-six and nine parts, or forty-five parts in all.

INDEX.

THE END.